BICYCLING.
MAGAZINE'S

Training Techniques for Cyclists

Greater Power, Faster Speed, Longer Endurance, Better Skills

EDITED BY ED PAVELKA

I1004350

Rodale Press, Inc.
Emmaus, Pennsylvania

Cover and Interior Designer: Susan P. Eugster
Cover Photographer: Sanford Schulwolf
Interior Photographers: Tim DeFrisco, Scott Markewitz, Pam Overend,
Beth Schneider, Kurt Wilson/Rodale Images

Library of Congress Cataloging-in-Publication Data

Bicycling magazine's training techniques for cyclists : greater power,
   faster speed, longer endurance, better skills / edited by Ed
   Pavelka.
          p.   cm.
     Includes index.
     ISBN 1–57954–168–2 paperback
     1. Cycling—Training.   I. Pavelka, Ed.   II. Bicycling magazine.
   III. Title: Training techniques for cyclists.
   GV1048.B54   1999
   796.6—dc21   99–36497

Distributed to the book trade by St. Martin's Press

2   4   6   8   10   9   7   5   3   1   paperback

Visit us on the Web at www.rodalesportsandfitness.com,
or call us toll-free at (800) 848-4735.

OUR PURPOSE

*We inspire and enable people to improve
their lives and the world around them.*

Notice

The information in this book is meant to supplement, not replace, proper road cycling and mountain biking training. Like any sport involving speed, equipment, balance, and environmental factors, cycling poses some inherent risk. The editors and publisher advise readers to take full responsibility for their safety and know their limits. Before practicing the skills described in this book, be sure that your equipment is well-maintained, and do not take risks beyond your experience, aptitude, training, and comfort level.

Contents

PART ONE

Key Concepts

PART TWO

Skills and Tactics

PART THREE

Coaches' Approaches

PART FOUR
Special Workouts

PART FIVE
Off-Season Training

Introduction

"People write and call and ask me to describe a general training week. But they don't need my general training week, they need their general training week. They need to figure their ideal training situation."

—NED OVEREND, WORLD-CHAMPION MOUNTAIN BIKE RACER

If you're ready to figure *your* ideal training situation, you've come to the right place. This book has the expert advice you need. As Ned Overend suggests, there is no universal program—the range of cycling goals and individual abilities is way too broad for that—but there are universal principles. By understanding them, you'll have what it takes to train smarter and more effectively than ever.

In the following pages are the best techniques used by some of cycling's most knowledgeable coaches. Although their hands-on experience is with racers, their recommendations work just as well for any rider who wants to boost his fitness and performance.

Careful readers may spot some inconsistent advice, especially when it comes to weight training. The reason, again, is that there is no one right way, a fact proven over and over by cyclists who have had outstanding success using different programs. What are presented here are the various experts' methods so you can choose those that fit your time, energy, and goals. Be confident that if you train consistently and with a purpose, great results will come.

PART ONE

Key Concepts

1
Pedaling like a Pro

You hear cycling coaches say it all the time: "Keep your cadence up. Learn how to spin." You're wasting time, they say, unless you're turning the crankarms about 90 rpm. Pedal at this magic number and you're riding like a pro.

Pedaling is so integral to being a strong, efficient rider that you need to address it before moving on to actual training techniques. Too many riders take pedaling for granted, thinking that it's just a matter of making their legs go up and down. Even a kid can do it, right? But like other things that seem simple, pedaling can be dramatically improved once you understand and practice its fine points.

Craig Griffin, a national cycling team coach, explains it well by saying, "Genetics determine how fast you can ride, but good pedal mechanics let you make the most of your gifts. If you can sit comfortably in the saddle at high rpm, you won't fade at the end of the ride, whether it's a track event or a century. By having the right technique, you can use a lower gear and a higher cadence, saving your legs for when it really counts."

Counting Cadence

Cadence, or rpm, is simply a measure of leg speed. Occasional riders tend to push a relatively high gear at 40 to 50 rpm, which feels natural and comfortable to them. But those who train for fitness and competition must learn to pedal twice as fast: between 80 and 110 rpm in moderate gears. Maintaining such a brisk cadence is called spinning.

It's easy to monitor your cadence while riding. Just count the number of times your right or left foot comes through its pedal stroke in 30 seconds, then multiply by two. The result is your pedaling rpm. Some cyclecomputers have a cadence sensor that counts rpm for you. This is so useful that national team riders are issued this type of computer at the Olympic Training Center in Colorado Springs. "They need to learn what the correct cadence feels like," Griffin says. "A computer provides immediate feedback." In time, you'll be able to accurately gauge your cadence without looking at the computer.

Keep in mind that a high cadence is best for top performance. There are several reasons for this. First, fast riding requires a high rate of work, and you're simply more efficient at a high cadence. By spinning moderate gears instead of pushing bigger ones to ride at a given speed, your leg muscles stay fresher and allow you to train more effectively. For example, you can do more intervals in a smaller gear with a higher cadence. This produces a higher heart rate and, eventually, superior cardiovascular fitness. Once this training adaptation occurs, your heart rate will actually be lower at any given speed. That's what efficiency is all about.

Second, and very important to racers, a high cadence facilitates rapid acceleration. The reason lies in the mechanics of pedaling. At low cadences in high gears, when a relatively great amount of force is required to turn the pedals, an increase in speed requires a substantial increase in effort. But at high cadences in moderate gears, not as much force is applied. It takes less time and effort to quicken cadence and accelerate. Think of it as driving with a manual transmission. If you want to increase speed quickly from 25 mph, you want to be in second gear rather than fourth gear. In the lower gear, the higher rpm makes the engine more responsive. But when you accelerate from lower rpm, the engine pickup is sluggish.

Third, pedaling at a fast cadence in a moderate gear requires less effort for each pedal stroke. The faster you spin, the less force is required to rotate the pedals. Thus, you can ride farther with less leg-muscle fatigue once your cardiovascular system can handle the challenge.

Finally, a fast cadence is easier on the knees. There are lots of cyclists who have suffered debilitating trauma from pushing too big a gear. Doing so results in a relatively forceful pedal stroke that loads the knees with constant strain, increasing the chance of injury.

Finding Your Perfect Cadence

Your ideal cadence depends on your type of riding. For instance, millions of Chinese who use their bicycles for daily transportation pedal merrily along at 40 to 50 rpm. Studies have proven this to be the most efficient cadence for the speeds they normally travel (about 10 mph).

However, for the reasons just discussed, athletic riders need a pedal rate of 90-plus rpm. In fact, some criterium racers cruise at 100 rpm or more because of the quick changes in speed that their event demands. Conversely, some big-gear time trialists can sustain a powerful stroke best when in the 80 to 85 rpm range. Fast recreational cyclists interested in fitness and doing well in low-key events such as centuries generally perform optimally in gears that let them spin continually at about 90 rpm.

Interestingly, the benefits of spinning begin to disappear above 100 rpm. While the reason is not fully understood, it's probable that such rapid leg movement begins to require proportionally more energy for the speed it produces. The main exception is during sprints, when cadences in big gears can top 120 rpm for a few seconds as riders obtain maximum speed.

To determine your most efficient cadence, do several 10-minute time trials, making sure to be equally rested before each one. Use your computer to keep your speed the same for all of them, but do each one in a different gear. This automatically changes your cadence. Monitor your rpm and heart rate. Your best cadence is the one that produces the fewest beats per minute. As training progresses and your fitness improves, you should see your heart rate go even lower when you're riding in this cadence range.

Keys to Better Pedaling

Here are several ways to develop a fast, fluid pedal stroke. When you have it right, you'll pedal in circles instead of like a yo-yo.

Set saddle height. You can't spin efficiently if your seat is too high or low. To check yours, measure your inseam length from crotch to floor while wearing socks. Hold the tape tight against your body and stand with your feet 6 inches apart. Multiply the resulting number by 0.883. This should be the distance between the center of the crankset axle and the top of the seat (make sure it's level), measured in line with the bike's seat tube. You'll tend to bounce at faster cadences, especially if your saddle is too high.

Wipe your shoes. Greg LeMond, the three-time Tour de France winner, is fond of saying that good pedaling action is like scraping mud off the soles of your shoes. If you imagine this, it helps eliminate the dead spot as your feet come through the bottom of the pedal circle. It helps you apply force longer and smooths the transition to the upstroke.

Raise your knees. Studies have proven that it's impossible to actually pull pedals up when spinning at a normal clip (as opposed to riding with a very slow cadence, such as on a steep climb). But what you can do is lighten the load on the upward pedal so that there's less weight for the opposite leg to push downward. World-champion mountain bike racer Ned Overend accomplishes this by visualizing his knees driving toward the handlebar. This pulls his pedals up the back side and across the top of the stroke, another potential dead spot. (For a related technique, see chapter 8.)

Ride rollers. As opposed to indoor trainers that hold your bike and do nothing to foster a smooth pedal stroke, rollers make you balance the bike. If your pedaling is choppy at higher cadences, you'll bounce right off. As you improve, put two pieces of tape about 6 inches apart on the front roller and strive to keep the wheel between them. When this becomes too easy, move the strips closer together.

Ride a fixed gear. By pedaling a bike that can't coast, your legs are forced to experience a wide range of cadences. Furthermore, the fact that the crankset moves your legs through the typical dead spots in the pedal circle helps ingrain a fluid, round leg action. You can ride a fixed-gear track bike on rollers or outside (if it's equipped with brakes) or rig a road bike into a fixed-gear machine. Check at a bike shop for technical assistance.

Spin the hills. On descents, keep your bike in a relatively low gear so you can boost your cadence to 110, 120, or more. Keep your hips and upper body still as your legs whip around. This takes both concentration and relaxation. When climbing, use gears that let you stay in the saddle, settle into a rhythm, and feel the entire pedal circle. Your cadence should be slow enough to let your brain keep up with your feet. Incorporate your hamstrings on the upstrokes by using Overend's knee-toward-bar technique. If there are no suitable hills in your area, you can get the same effects by using tailwinds and headwinds while deliberately under- or over-gearing.

2

The Importance of Max VO$_2$

You're weaving up a steep hill at almost maximum effort, unsure whether you're going to make it. Suddenly, another rider cruises past. In a moment, he reaches the top and disappears. Astonished and a bit demoralized, you wonder about his secret. Is he eating some miracle food? Is he taking a performance-enhancing drug? Is his bike that much lighter than yours?

These things rarely are the reason. In a situation like this, it's almost certain that the rider's big advantage is a higher max VO$_2$.

Max VO$_2$ is shorthand for maximal oxygen consumption, the amount of oxygen that the body can extract from the air during all-out exercise. It's a way of defining aerobic capacity, so it's used to judge potential in endurance sports such as cycling, running, swimming, and cross-country skiing. The symbol is derived from the volume (V) of oxygen (O$_2$) used per minute.

Oxygen is transported by your blood to all of your body's tissues. During exercise, more than 90 percent of the oxygen in your blood is used by the working muscles. There it meets with carbohydrate and fat molecules derived from food. The oxygen transforms these molecules into usable power, or energy. In essence, then, max VO$_2$ is a measurement of how well you turn the air you breathe into energy. The higher your max VO$_2$, the better your cycling performance should be.

The most accurate way to measure max VO$_2$ is through a sophisticated lab test. It's very demanding because it requires riding a stationary bicycle until exhaustion. You maintain a specified cadence while pedaling resistance is increased at regular intervals. When your cadence starts slowing no matter how hard you try, you're done. To make this even more fun, you wear a mask or mouthpiece with a nose clamp. A tube carries your expired air to a machine that analyzes it for oxygen content and ultimately determines your max VO$_2$.

The cost for this test is usually $100 or more at hospitals or human-performance labs. Consider it a worthwhile investment if you're serious about understanding and maximizing your cycling potential.

VO$_2$ Values

On average, a highly trained male pro cyclist has a max VO$_2$ of 65 to 75. This figure represents the milliliters of oxygen per kilogram of body weight that are delivered to working muscles in one minute. Looked at another way, a 180-pound (82-kilogram) cyclist with a max VO$_2$ of 65 uses 5,330 milliliters of oxygen (82 kilogram × 65 milliliter) during a 60-second maximal aerobic effort. That's amazing, considering that the same person needs just 287 milliliters per minute when resting. Max

VO_2 values for extremely fit females usually measure between 50 and 60. Typical couch-potato levels range from 35 to 45.

Great cyclists are extremely well-conditioned, of course, but they probably are also genetically endowed with a high aerobic capacity. For the rest of us, who operate well below our ultimate physiological potential, max VO_2 can be improved through training. For instance, it's repeatedly been shown that untrained beginning cyclists can increase their max VO_2's by 15 to 20 percent in just three to four months of regular riding.

Once fitness has been boosted to a relatively high level, however, improvement becomes more difficult. Even if you train consistently all season, your max VO_2 may improve by just 4 or 5 percent. Conversely, complete inactivity for three weeks may cost you about 30 percent of your aerobic capacity. Fortunately, you can regain most of this in 10 days of regular training, and all of it in 30 days.

Boosting Your Max

Intensity is the key to enhancing aerobic capacity. To increase max VO_2, emphasize the quality of your training rather than the quantity. Each week, schedule one or two high-intensity rides such as intervals. For example, go hard for 60 or 90 seconds, recover for the same length of time by spinning an easy gear, then go again. Repeat this 5 to 10 times to get the type of stress that improves your ability to consume oxygen. Another way is to climb hills, which automatically boosts your heart rate and oxygen consumption to high levels.

Want a less physically painful way? Lose weight. Remember, the max VO_2 formula is milliliters of oxygen per kilogram of body weight per minute. Because a divisor is weight, if all else remains the same and you lose a few pounds, your max VO_2 goes up. Regular riding will help you burn body fat as it boosts aerobic fitness.

The Payoff

Here's the good news: By raising your max VO_2, you'll become a better cyclist. Unfortunately, raising it by 10 percent doesn't mean you'll see a 10 percent improvement in your riding performance. Instead, the increase may be less than half of that. The reason for this is air resistance. The faster you ride, the tougher the invisible wall and the more energy you need to push through it. For instance, going from 20 to 25 mph is about 30 percent harder than going from 15 to 20 mph. Climbing, which takes place at slower speeds and depends greatly on aerobic conditioning, correlates more directly.

But even a small annual improvement becomes significant over time. And remember that max VO_2 is just one aspect of cycling performance. As you increase aerobic capacity, you also enhance muscle strength, pedaling technique, and bike-handling skills. Alone, each may produce only a slight improvement. Together, they can spell the difference between being passed on hills and doing the passing.

3
Target Heart Rate

Let's say you ride six times per week for a total of 10 hours. A friend cycles just four times per week and logs 7 hours. Who is improving their fitness more?

The answer is not as simple as it seems. In fact, your friend could be making significantly more progress. The reason lies in what these numbers don't tell—how hard each of you is riding. Along with frequency and duration, intensity is an essential component in determining the effectiveness of training rides.

While the number and length of rides are easily measured, intensity is more difficult to gauge. To determine it, you must know the amount of effort you're using compared to the maximum you could generate if you were working as hard as possible.

Fortunately, you have a built-in intensity meter that always reports this information. It's your heart rate. It ranges from a minimum value when you're resting to a maximum level during all-out efforts. When you ride, your heart rate usually fluctuates through a wide range but is almost always below 100 percent. The percentage of maximum accurately reflects your exercise intensity. For instance, if your heart rate is at 80 percent of maximum, you're riding at 80 percent intensity.

Most exercise physiologists agree that to significantly increase fitness, you must maintain an intensity level of at least 65 percent. This value has come to be known as target heart rate. Although simple, this concept is used even by elite cyclists. To increase fitness, most of their training starts at this level. Subsequent chapters will discuss how heart rate is used to define several training zones above 65 percent (and one below that level) in order to produce specific performance benefits. But even if you do nothing more than use the following basic guidelines, your rides are guaranteed to make you fitter.

Find Your Maximum

Before you can calculate your target heart rate, you need to determine your maximum. There are several ways. First, you can take a medically supervised stress test or a max VO_2 test that measures maximal oxygen consumption. These are very accurate but expensive, so recreational riders will probably want to consider one of the next two alternatives.

At one extreme is a simple formula: Subtract your age from 220. If you're 35, for instance, the result is 185—the theoretical maximum number of beats per minute (bpm) your heart can attain. But beware. Among the general cycling population, this formula is known to be inaccurate by as many as 10 or 15 bpm in either direction. For example, one 52-year-old rider had a lab-tested maximum of 180, a significant departure from the formula's predicted max of 168. If he were to base his target heart rate on the lower number, his training would not be nearly as effective.

Perhaps the best method is to use a long, steep hill. Be well-rested, warm up sufficiently, then ride to the top like you're sprinting for a world championship. Push, push, push!

It's impossible to take your pulse accurately in this situation, so you need a heart-rate monitor (HRM), which you can use later for regular training. HRMs start at about $70, depending on features. Get the type with a wireless transmitter that straps to your chest. The monitor should let you set audible upper and lower pulse limits. Also useful is a memory that stores your heart rate at set intervals throughout a ride. Later, you can analyze how much time you spent at various levels. Some HRMs interface with personal computers to store information and generate graphs.

(*Note:* Before subjecting yourself to the exertion of a max-heart-rate test, get your doctor's approval. This is especially necessary if you are over 35, overweight, sedentary, or have any cardiac problems. To avoid medical risks, use the 220-minus-age formula.)

Determine Your Zone

Once you have your maximum, determine your target range by calculating the beats per minute that represent 65 and 80 percent. In other
words, multiply your max by 0.65 and 0.80. For example, let's say your
HRM displays 190 bpm at the top of that all-out hill. Your target range
is between 124 bpm (190 × 0.65) and 152 bpm (190 × 0.80). Whenever
you're in this zone—no matter how you're riding or even what sport
you're participating in—you are training intensely enough to improve
cardiovascular fitness. The closer you are to 80 percent, the more benefit
you derive.

Attack Fat

There's a common belief that you burn more body fat with low-intensity training. The truth is, at lower intensities fat does provide a high
percentage of fuel. But overall, you can burn more fat calories by riding
harder.

For example, cycling for one hour at a heart rate of 120 bpm may
burn 350 calories. Of these, about half (175) will be fat calories. Conversely, if you pedal harder and get your heart rate to 160 bpm, you may
burn 1,000 calories in an hour. At this intensity, only about one-fifth
(200) will be fat calories, but that's still 25 more calories than with the
low-intensity ride. So overall, you burn slightly more fat calories and
nearly three times as many total calories at the higher intensity.

This is doubly significant because of the way your body restocks calories. Studies show that when you exercise below your target zone and
burn a high percentage of fat calories, your body replenishes these first.
So you're back where you started. For losing body fat, it's best to ride at
the highest level that's comfortably sustainable. Don't restrict intensity in
the mistaken belief that it's necessary in order to burn more fat.

Monitor Your Training Intensity

There's little doubt that the harder you train, the more you improve.
There's also a point of diminishing returns, however. Training above 80
percent of maximum is stressful and, if done too frequently, will result
in overtraining and poor form. It's hard to go wrong by riding in a
target range of 65 to 80 percent of maximum. This won't bring you to
ultimate cycling fitness, but it's safe and effective if your goals are better
performance and weight control.

4
Lactate Threshold

You're flying down the road in a group of riders. The pace is hard but tolerable. Your heart rate is well below maximum. Then a strong rider moves to the front, and the pace quickens. Uh-oh—now you have a choice. You can drop to the back or increase your effort and stay with the pack. You go for it.

At first, you can handle the extra effort. But soon your breathing rate increases dramatically—almost to the point of panting. Then your legs start feeling heavy and even your arms begin to ache. You must slow down.

What happened? Were you in the wrong gear? Are the other riders that much better? Were you just having an off day? The answer, most likely, is none of the above. You simply crossed your lactate threshold.

LT, as it's commonly called, is your body's breaking point during exercise. Before you reach it, most of your energy is produced aerobically (with oxygen). But after you exceed it, a significant amount of your energy is produced anaerobically (without oxygen). Anaerobic exercise produces a substance known as lactic acid. This acid accumulates in your blood and working muscles, disrupting their balance. You feel this happening through such symptoms as breathlessness and muscle burn.

Because of its association with anaerobic metabolism, this point has for years been called the anaerobic threshold, or AT. This term is misleading, however, because at AT you aren't yet anaerobic, and the whole mechanism is based on accumulation of lactic acid. This makes lactate threshold the more accurate description.

You may also come across new terms such as MLSS for "maximum lactate at steady state" or ONBL for "onset of blood lactate." All of this academic jargon means the same thing—your muscles catch fire and you start breathing like a steam engine. As soon as this happens, your ability to continue at the same intensity is very limited.

On the positive side, you can develop the fitness it takes to sustain a fast pace longer if you train at a level right around your LT. This is the guiding principle behind much of the training that the pros do. In one study, several fit cyclists were able to ride intensely for 50 minutes by staying slightly below their respective LTs. However, not one was able to continue for more than 20 minutes after crossing the threshold.

Finding Your LT

The most reliable way to pinpoint LT is at a hospital or human-performance laboratory equipped for max-VO_2 testing. Such labs will find your breaking point either by analyzing the air you exhale or by drawing blood while you exercise to check lactic acid concentration. But it's also possible to estimate your LT using methods that rely on the less accurate correlation between heart rate and LT.

One formula is similar to ballparking your maximum heart rate. It's done by subtracting your age from 220, then multiplying that number by 0.85. The result is an estimation of the heart rate at which you reach LT. Or, if you know your maximum heart rate, simply multiply it by 0.85.

Another, more exact method is called Test Conconi (named after an Italian cycling doctor). To do it, you need a cyclecomputer, heart-rate monitor, stopwatch, stationary trainer to put your bike on, and someone to record data for you. After warming up, select a fairly large gear that you won't spin out on by the end of the test. Pedal for one minute at 10 mph and record your heart rate. Increase your speed by 1 mph, and record heart rate again 1 minute later. Continue. You're done when you can no longer hold your speed for a full minute.

Now you can use all of these numbers to make a graph. On the vertical axis, put heart beats per minute. On the horizontal axis, put speed. (The graph is clearer if you do this as speed cubed, or mph $\times$ mph $\times$ mph.) Plot each point from your test and connect the dots. The resulting line should incline steadily, then suddenly bend sharply toward horizontal. According to Conconi, this bend pinpoints your LT.

The Connection to Max VO$_2$

Lactate threshold and max VO_2 are not the same. Max VO_2 represents your aerobic power, or the maximum amount of oxygen you can extract from the air while exercising. Interestingly, you reach your LT long before you reach your max VO_2. Thus, LT is often measured as a percentage of max VO_2. For instance, lactic acid may start to accumulate and you may begin producing a significant amount of energy without oxygen at 50 percent of your max VO_2.

Which of these measurements is more important? Your LT represents the maximum intensity that you can sustain for a reasonably long period, such as during a time trial. Max VO_2 has less practical value, though it's certainly important for predicting your potential in an aerobic activity such as cycling. You reach max VO_2 only during the last few moments of intense effort, and you can't sustain it. For this reason, most physiologists consider LT to be a more useful number in terms of cycling performance. The higher your LT, the harder you can ride for extended periods. An improvement in LT correlates directly to improved performance—and a better chance of staying with a fast pack.

For untrained people, typical LT values are 40 to 70 percent of max VO_2, with the average being around 55 percent. As a cyclist, your threshold will be higher. Pro racers may have LTs as high as 85 percent of max VO_2.

Improving LT

Just as training can improve your max VO_2, it can also raise your LT. That's the goal—narrowing the gap between your LT heart rate and your maximum heart rate. It's been demonstrated many times that long, fast rides as well as interval training can elevate your LT. For instance, one study found that training rides done at 85 to 90 percent of max heart rate can improve a new cyclist's lactate threshold as much as 70 percent in just 9 weeks. Another study showed dramatic LT improvements from doing 10 2-minute intervals 3 days a week at just slightly below the maximum intensity that could be sustained for the duration of the effort.

The bottom line is that training at or slightly above your lactate threshold is the best way to raise it and develop the ability to ride longer near it.

5
Overtraining

You've undoubtedly heard of overtraining. It's something that happens to elite cyclists who hammer out 600-mile weeks, race in cold rain, and then cap it off with the Tour de France. How could it happen to those who are lucky to get in five or six hours of riding a week?

Believe it—you could fall victim to the big O, and it's easier than you think. It's the total stress load in your life that counts, not just time on the bike, according to Ed Burke, Ph.D., cycling physiologist and director of the exercise-science program at the University of Colorado at Colorado Springs. As far as your body is concerned, training is just another stress.

Pro cyclists routinely ride 20 to 25 hours per week—but that's all they do. Life's little details are handled by team management. Now look at your schedule. If you're like most people, you work 40 or more hours per week, ride herd on kids, juggle a budget, shop, mow the lawn—and try to wedge in time for rides. The stress you're under may very well be more intense than what the pros face.

Depths of Fatigue

Cycling has the reputation of being a sport for tough guys, and the toughest never utter the word "overtrained." For them, nagging fatigue is a phenomenon of the mind and not the legs. The solution is simple: Ride through it.

Ann Snyder, Ph.D., director of the exercise-physiology lab at the University of Wisconsin-Milwaukee, met a bunch of these tough guys and decided to find out how stalwart they really were. For 2 weeks, she subjected them to more than 10 hours of interval training per week, plus races on weekends. One rider couldn't sustain the load and quit the study after 6 days. Seven of them survived. By the end, only one was able to finish a race.

The findings? All of the subjects displayed a downturn in performance, as indicated by time-trial and power-output tests. Sleeping heart rate increased, while max heart rate and max VO_2 (maximal oxygen consumption) decreased. Also, subjective responses to a questionnaire showed a deterioration in the riders' "general state of well-being."

In other words, they were cooked.

But there also was a positive development. After a 2-week rest period in which the training load was roughly halved, performance reached its former level or exceeded it. This raises one of the central dilemmas of training: Hard work makes cyclists stronger, but how much is too much? And how long does it take to recover and experience this rebound effect?

Overreaching

Exercise physiologists prefer to make a distinction between overtraining, which is debilitating and long-term (lasting weeks or months), and overreaching, which is what you feel at the end of a particularly hard week of riding. With adequate recovery, overreaching makes you faster and stronger. Unfortunately, there's no distinct border between the two states. And either way, it's dangerous country to be in.

Although several riders in Dr. Snyder's hardy bunch eventually improved, it didn't happen until after they suffered the physiological distress measured by two performance markers.

1. Time trials. Riders raced a 5-mile course once per week. Times slowed significantly—by about 41 seconds in the week after intense training. Also, riders couldn't attain the same heart rate that they did in the first time trial.

2. Maximum power output. Cyclists performed a weekly ergometer test on a stationary bicycle, in which the load increased by 50 watts every 5 minutes until exhaustion. Power output declined an average of 26 watts after the intensive training.

Of all of Snyder's measurements, the only ones that didn't change were weight and body-fat percentage.

Reducing the Risk

If, despite the obvious risks, you decided to embark on a similar period of intense training, or overreaching, how long must you rest before you can reap the benefits? Dr. Snyder's study supplied some answers. The two key performance variables (time trials and power output) continued to improve throughout the 2-week recovery period. In other words, the typical two or three days of tapering before an important event may not be enough. Although the study ended after 2 weeks of recovery, the findings suggest that performance may have continued to improve with even more rest.

Cyclists may be especially prone to overtraining. In fact, few other sports seem capable of inducing such a bone-deep weariness. This may be due to the concentrated way that cycling stresses the body, according to Dr. Snyder. "Cyclists' muscles can become overtrained sooner because they're using mainly the quadriceps," she said. "Runners use more muscle mass. With cyclists, if the quads are tired, the rider will be tired."

And remember, you needn't undergo a titanic workload to become overtrained. "Less experienced athletes and those who coach themselves may be particularly prone," according to a sports-medicine journal, because they either emulate the programs of elite riders or fail to recognize the symptoms of overtraining. In other words, it's all relative. Your 100-mile week might be a postrace recovery for former world champion and Olympian Lance Armstrong, but if you averaged only 30 miles during previous weeks, your body could show all the symptoms of overtraining.

Warning Signs

How do you guard against overtraining? While most riders don't have access to the sophisticated measuring methods used by physiologists, you can still monitor a few key indicators.

Resting heart rate. Most cycling coaches emphasize this. Record your pulse each morning shortly after waking, using the same routine to ensure consistent conditions. Beware when you're suddenly six to eight beats above normal. You'd be smart to forgo any hard training that you had planned.

Time-trial performance. Dr. Snyder recommends doing a short time trial in similar conditions every other week as you train toward a big event. "I wouldn't worry about a time that's a few seconds slower," she says. "But if you're off by a minute, it could be due to overtraining."

Time-trial heart rate. A drop of 10 beats per minute (bpm) or so in your average heart rate can indicate overtraining. (Some monitors make this easy to check by calculating the average for you.) There's real danger if your resting heart rate is rising while your bpm during hard efforts is falling. This narrowing of the gap may be the most telling symptom that you're cooked.

Power. When a workload is overwhelming your body, you actually get weaker. In a study of cyclists doing hard intervals two or three times per day for 2 weeks, max power output deteriorated quickly. You may notice this on climbs when you find yourself using lower gears than usual.

Disposition. While this may seem the vaguest possible index, it may be one of the most reliable. In one study involving swimmers, measurements of such things as anger, depression, and vigor worsened markedly when training loads were doubled. So when every pothole seems like a personal insult, beware. Apathy is another warning sign. If you used to get fired up just thinking about riding but now you can't drag yourself off the couch, you're probably overtrained.

Nagging ailments. If you get successive colds, suspect overtraining. Studies have shown that your immune system is compromised during periods of high stress, and upper-respiratory infections are often the result. Another signal is that saddle sores and minor wounds are slow to heal. If you crash and a month later your wound is still oozing, back off until your body can heal itself.

Stagnant performance. The goal of training is to ride faster or longer in your targeted events. If after a period of hard work you show no performance benefit, you may not have rested enough. Moreover, if you continue to ride hard in the face of this evidence, you'll probably end up overtrained.

Bouncing Back

So you're feeling puny and are exhibiting the symptoms described above. What's the remedy? There's only one, and you won't like it: rest. Abusing your body got you into this fix, and only some time off—mentally and physically—will set things right. Hang up the bike for a week or more.

When you resume riding, cut your usual volume and intensity by half for at least another week. Then increase your distance or pace by no more than 10 percent per week. And try to reduce the other stresses in your life.

As Dr. Snyder found, "Overreaching could be part of a normal training cycle. If you rest for a few days, you'll recover. But with overtraining, it could require a month or two. That's the difference. The bottom line is that both will lead to detriments in performance unless you take days off."

Rest. It could be the toughest training choice you ever make.

6
The Cyclist's Diet

Confused about nutrition? That's not surprising. With all the conflicting advice going around, probably the only people who aren't confused are the ones who aren't paying attention. There are constant claims that some food or diet will help people live longer, lose weight, look younger . . . even ride better.

If you're tired of feeling perplexed—and perhaps bouncing from one food fad to another, only to learn the hard way that radical eating plans, magic ingredients, and expensive supplements don't work—this chapter is for you. It contains all you need to know about eating for good health and better cycling performance. No hype or empty promises, just the facts.

The Case for Carbohydrate

If you had a plate of pasta for every article you've ever seen about carbohydrate, you could probably start your own Italian restaurant. There's good reason, however, why sports nutritionists hype carb: It's your best fuel.

Essentially, carbohydrate is sugar. Simple carbohydrate is a single or double sugar molecule—usually glucose, fructose, galactose, sucrose, or lactose. These are found in nutritious foods (fruits, for instance) as well as in less healthful fare such as candy. Complex carbohydrate is a long chain of simple sugars and is often called a starch. Potatoes and pasta are good examples.

When you eat carb, it's broken down and converted to blood glucose, the body's main fuel and the only type that can feed the brain. Glucose that's not immediately used for energy is stored in the muscles and liver as glycogen and used later for fuel. If these storage spots are full, the glucose is converted to fat.

Carbohydrate is a better cycling fuel than protein or fat. Although stored protein can be converted to energy when glucose and glycogen become depleted, the process is inefficient. Stored fat can also be a fuel source, but it can't be converted to energy in the absence of glucose. This is why you need carbohydrate. Not only does a diet that's high in fat and protein carry more calories and adverse health effects but it also does a poorer job of providing energy for cycling.

Carb Formula

During and immediately after a hard effort, simple and complex carbs are equally effective as fuel. But in your general diet, it's best to emphasize the complex type, which promotes significantly greater glycogen synthesis and offers vitamins, minerals, and fiber along with the energy.

Overall, nutritionists recommend that at least 60 percent of your calories come from carbohydrate. For cyclists and other aerobic athletes, 65 percent is better. Food packages list carb content as a percentage of daily calories, making your intake fairly simple to track. To help, here's a formula that enables you to estimate the number of carb grams that account for 65 percent of your diet.

First, determine your total calorie requirement by multiplying your weight by 15. To this number, add 10 calories (for men) or 8 calories (for women) for each minute of cycling you do each day. The total is roughly the number of daily calories you need to maintain your weight. (To lose weight, consume 500 fewer calories each day. You'll lose 1 pound per week.)

For example, a 150-pound man who does a 1-hour training ride would figure as follows: 150 × 15 = 2,250 calories + 600 calories (10 calories × 60 minutes) = 2,850 total calories. For this rider, 65 percent of total calories amounts to about 1,850 (2,850 total calories × 0.65 = 1,852.5). This is the number of carb calories he should eat daily. Because carb has 4 calories per gram, he can divide 1,850 by four to determine that he needs about 460 grams of carb a day (1,850 carb calories ÷ 4 calories per gram = 462.5 grams of carbohydrate).

Beyond the math, the point is that you should increase your intake of whole-grain breads, nonfat dairy products, cereals, pasta, rice, potatoes, vegetables, fruits, and juices. At the same time, keep your total daily calorie consumption at the right level by decreasing your intake of fat and protein as found in meat, cheese, whole dairy products, and snack foods.

Extending Endurance

No matter how well-trained you are, your endurance is limited by one thing: the depletion of stored glycogen. When glycogen is depleted, you become light-headed, dizzy, and fatigued. In cycling, it's called bonking. Fortunately, it isn't inevitable. There are ways to increase your glycogen stores and prolong performance.

The best way is through training. Well-conditioned muscles can store 20 to 50 percent more glycogen than untrained ones. To take advantage of this expanded capacity, you need to eat plenty of carb calories every day. Successive days of low intake can lead to a condition called training glycogen depletion, characterized by fatigue and lackluster performance.

For several days before an important event, pack your muscles with glycogen by reducing your riding and increasing your intake of carbohydrate to as much as 75 percent of total calories. By making more glycogen available to your muscles—and using less—you'll top off your tank for the big ride. If you have trouble consuming enough food to get all the carbohydrate you need, try a concentrated sports drink known as a carbo-loader, which can supply more than 200 grams of carbohydrate per serving.

Liquid Carb

Even the world's strongest cyclist would run out of gas if he didn't refuel while riding. The reason is simple. Early in a ride, almost all of your energy comes from stored muscle glycogen. But as glycogen levels decline, you rely more on blood glucose for fuel. To continue riding, you need to keep these sugar levels high.

One way to do this is with an energy drink. If a drink contains too much carbohydrate, however, it bogs down in your stomach and takes too long to reach your bloodstream, which results in dehydration and possibly nausea. The most effective drinks contain just enough carbohydrate (5 to 7 percent) to empty into the bloodstream quickly, extending performance without interfering with hydration.

Some cyclists can drink fruit juice (perhaps diluted with water) or use commercial drinks with high (up to 25 percent) carb concentrations without problems. The benefit is a bigger dose of energy per bottle. When preparing a drink, you may want to try different concentrations to find the strongest one that causes no problems. Of course, experiment during training rides, not in important events.

To be effective, an energy drink should deliver about 40 to 60 grams of carbohydrate per hour. Check the ingredients and consider avoiding products that contain fructose (many do). This is a slow-absorbing sugar that causes stomach distress in some riders. Look instead for sucrose, glucose, or glucose polymers. The last consist of several glucose molecules linked together. This chain is absorbed quickly, as if it were a single molecule, but it breaks up in your bloodstream to give you the benefit of several glucose molecules instead of just one.

For rides longer than 2½ to 3 hours, you also need solid food. There are numerous commercial energy bars to choose from, plus good high-carb foods such as bagels, bananas, or dried fruits. Unlike drinks, these choices do not enhance hydration, so drink plenty of water with them.

A Matter of Fat

Next to carbohydrate, fat is your body's best fuel. It's particularly useful on long, steady rides when intensity is low. But don't assume that this gives you license to eat all the ice cream and french fries you want.

True, body fat is important for storing vitamins and providing insulation. But in excess, it's one of the biggest health risks imaginable. It increases susceptibility to heart disease, high blood pressure, certain cancers, and diabetes.

Most people have plenty of stored fat and, in fact, most have too much. While humans can store only limited amounts of glycogen, we can stockpile unlimited fat. Remember, though, that fat can be burned only in the presence of glucose. For these reasons, people need more carbohydrate, not more fat.

Any kind of food can turn into body fat if you eat too much. But not surprisingly, the most likely source of body fat is dietary fat. Compared with protein and carbohydrate, dietary fat has more than twice as many calories (nine per gram rather than four), and it appears to be stored more readily.

For optimal health and performance, nutritionists recommend that you derive no more than 30 percent of your total calories from fat and no more than 10 percent from the saturated fat found primarily in animal products. The remainder should be the unsaturated form that comes from vegetable oils, nuts, and grains.

One way to ensure a low fat intake is to check nutrition labels and select foods with less than 3 grams of fat per 100 calories. If this information isn't plainly listed, you can calculate the fat percentage this way: Look on the label for the grams of fat per serving. Multiply this number by nine, then divide the result by the calories per serving. The result is the percentage of calories from fat. For example, one serving of a popular cheese spread has 80 calories and 6 grams of fat. So, 6 grams of fat × 9 calories per gram of fat = 54 fat calories; and 54 fat calories ÷ 80 total calories = 67.5 percent calories from fat.

To figure a food's percentage of calories from carbohydrate or protein, multiply the number of grams by four instead of nine. Then divide by total calories.

Trim fat from your diet by reducing your intake of animal foods. When you do eat them, select lean cuts of meat, skinless poultry, and nonfat dairy products. Cut down on butter, margarine, salad dressings, and hydrogenated and tropical oils (found in many baked goods).

Interestingly, the fitter you are, the better you burn fat. A well-trained body is capable of delivering more oxygen to the muscles, thus increasing the rate of fat metabolism and sparing some glycogen stores.

Shedding Pounds

Are you looking for long-term weight loss that will improve your cycling performance? Then trash the crash diets. Sure, some weight (mostly water and lean body mass) may come off quickly, but it usually returns just as fast.

To take off fat—and keep it off—you must make two permanent (and almost painless) lifestyle commitments. The first is easy: exercise. Make time to ride. Don't let yourself go more than two days without it. Studies have shown that you can stay trim with as little as 3 hours of exercise per week.

The second commitment is harder: cut calories. The best way isn't eating less, but reducing fat intake. In the average American diet, nearly 40 percent of all calories come from fat. Trim this to 20 to 30 percent, and you're almost guaranteed to lose weight.

Remember, fat is twice as calorie-dense as protein or carbohydrate. So as long as your foods aren't fatty, you can eat plenty and still keep your calorie intake relatively low. For example, in a study at Cornell University in Ithaca, New York, subjects were put on either a 40 percent or 15 percent fat diet and allowed to eat all they wanted. Both groups ate similar amounts, but those in the 15 percent group averaged 700 fewer daily calories.

Plenty of Protein

Cyclists do require more protein than sedentary people. But this doesn't mean you have to increase your protein intake. In fact, you're probably already getting more than you need.

One reason that cyclists need extra protein is for fuel. Once muscles have depleted their primary energy source (carbohydrate), they begin using protein. "Protein can be a small but significant source of energy—about 5 to 10 percent of total energy needs," according to researcher Michael J. Zackin, Ph.D., of the University of Massachusetts Medical School in Worcester. "Protein calories become increasingly important in carbohydrate-depleted states. If you train more than an hour a day and begin to deplete glycogen stores, you become increasingly dependent on body protein for energy."

Although results vary widely, Dr. Zackin says cycling may raise your protein requirements 20 to 90 percent beyond the U.S. Recommended Dietary Allowance (RDA). The RDA is 0.363 gram of protein per pound of body weight. For a 150-pound man, this is about 54 grams per day. For a 120-pound woman, it's about 44 grams. Add the 20 to 90 percent, and the male cyclist's daily protein need rises to between 65 and 103 grams, and the woman's to 53 to 84 grams.

That may seem like a lot, but most active people are already at these levels or beyond. This was illustrated in a study of eight highly trained women cyclists. Though their diets fell short of recommended values for several nutrients, their protein intake was 145 percent of the RDA. High protein levels simply aren't hard to reach. For instance, 3 ounces of meat, fish, or poultry contain 21 grams of protein. A cup of beans has 14 grams, 3 tablespoons of peanut butter has 12, and a cup of nonfat milk contains 9. All of this adds up quickly. In fact, the average American consumes 100 grams of protein per day.

So unless you're a strict vegetarian or chronic dieter, you probably don't need to increase your protein intake. Instead, worry about where your protein comes from. The best sources are low in fat and include a healthy dose of complex carbohydrate. Muscles are built by work, not by extra protein, and work is best fueled by carbohydrate. Some low-fat, high-protein choices include whole grains, beans, vegetables, fish, skinless poultry, soy products, lean cuts of meat, and nonfat dairy products. Even vegetarians can get plenty of high-quality protein with a varied diet combining grains, legumes, nuts, seeds, vegetables, dairy products, and eggs. Overall, nutritionists say about 15 percent of your diet should be protein calories.

Amino Acid Supplements

Protein helps build muscle tissue, and protein is nothing more than a strand of amino acids. This is why many athletes take amino acid supplements. The theory is that by augmenting your diet with pills or powders, you build muscle. In reality, though, this doesn't work.

Because most people get more than enough protein in their diets, few have amino acid deficiencies. Any excess, whether it comes from food or heavily hyped supplements, is burned inefficiently as a fuel or turned into fat, not muscle. In great excess, amino acid supplements can even lead to dehydration, calcium loss, and liver or kidney damage.

Even if extra amino acids were beneficial, the best way to get them isn't through pills or powders. As with vitamins, the best source is food. In fact, on an average day, most people ingest tens of thousands of milligrams of amino acids.

"Most supplements provide 200 to 500 mg of amino acids per pill, while an ounce of chicken supplies 7,000 mg," says nutritionist Ellen Coleman, author of *Eating for Endurance*, adding that chicken also supplies other essential nutrients. In addition, getting the same amount of amino acids from supplements as you would from an ounce of chicken may cost as much as 20 times more.

Vitamins and Minerals

As with amino acids, if you're eating a well-balanced diet, you almost certainly get all of the vitamins and minerals you need. A cyclist's vitamin and mineral requirements "are no greater than those of a sedentary person," according to Coleman. Vitamin supplements do not provide a direct source of energy. "Their only purpose is to help people with nutritional deficiencies stemming from poor diets."

No research has found that taking supplements improves performance in well-nourished cyclists. On the other hand, some substances can actually accumulate in your body to dangerous levels if taken in large quantities. Too much niacin, for example, can cause rashes, nausea, and diarrhea. It can also interfere with your body's ability to burn fat for fuel. This forces you to use glycogen at a faster rate, which makes you fatigue more quickly during a ride.

At about a dime per dose, a daily vitamin and mineral supplement is often viewed as cheap insurance. So go ahead and take one if you want to be sure all bases are covered. But if you're feeling tired or your performance is slipping, don't expect a supplement to help. The cause is probably overtraining or eating too little carbohydrate, not the lack of some vitamin. "When people feel better after taking vitamin and mineral supplements, it's usually due to the strength of their belief that they'll help," Coleman notes.

PART TWO

Skills
and Tactics

7
Breathing

You say you already know how to breathe? Think again.

It's not your pedaling muscles alone that get you down the road. Breathing supplies the oxygen that makes those well-trained quadriceps work. But many cyclists don't control the simple act of respiration. They don't know how to breathe efficiently. As a result, they waste energy and gasp uncomfortably on climbs.

One place where this becomes very apparent is at high altitude. Colorado's Skip Hamilton, a masters champion and national-class endurance athlete, frequently coaches at cycling camps in the Rocky Mountains. He often sees sea-level cyclists laboring up the 10,000-foot passes, gasping like beached fish. That's the perfect time for him to ride alongside and explain how to get more out of every breath. His favorite technique, called switch-side breathing, produces almost miraculous increases in climbing speed and comfort—and it's easy to learn. Hamilton picked it up from Ian Jackson, author of the book *BreathPlay*, during snowshoe runs around Aspen. Then he started using it on the bike.

No one is quite sure why switch-side breathing helps, but there are some clues. Hamilton recalls noticing how often a runner's injuries occur on the same side of the body. For instance, a person's right knee, ankle, and hamstring may all hurt. Furthermore, these injuries usually coincide with the runner's dominant breathing side—right-side injuries when the person has a habit of breathing in rhythm with right-foot strikes. Then, when that runner learns to switch-side breathe, injuries fade away. Apparently, if you always breathe on one side, you may subconsciously exert more effort on that side. On the bike, switch-side breathing equalizes leg force and this, in turn, makes climbing easier.

Belly Breathing

Start learning switch-side breathing by practicing correct athletic breathing when you're off the bike. Lie on your back on the floor with a book on your stomach. Breathe in slowly and fully, expanding your diaphragm, not your chest. The book should move toward the ceiling. Then exhale steadily so it sinks toward the floor.

Most people think deep breathing means expanding their chests, huffing and puffing like a drill sergeant. But if you look at profile photos of professional cyclists, they almost look fat. Their midsections are nearly the circumference of their chests. Their diaphragms are conditioned to expand like bullfrogs in full voice. It may look funny—but it leaves more room for air to get into the lungs.

Most riders exhale on the same side of the pedal stroke every single time. If you're right-handed, you probably breathe out when the right pedal starts the downstroke. You can check by climbing a flight of stairs and paying attention to your pattern of in- and out-breaths. Once you get a rhythm going, it's almost a sure bet that you exhale each time the same foot hits a step.

The easiest way to change this pattern of same-side breathing is simply to take an extra-long out-breath every 5 to 10 pedal strokes. This automatically switches your out-breath to the other downstroke. Practice doing it on long climbs, and it will soon become second nature. You can even practice off the bike by climbing stairs in a stadium or tall building. When you're stairclimbing, your foot strike is slower and more pronounced than in cycling, so it's easier to coordinate it with your breathing.

The final element is emphasizing out-breaths. If you exhale with force, you won't even need to think about breathing in. It will happen automatically. Some riders go as far as making a guttural sound like a weight lifter each time they breathe out during hard climbing. You may sound like a pig in a poke (or a pig getting poked), but it works.

8
Isolated Leg Training

What if there were a simple training technique that could improve all aspects of your cycling fitness? It could increase your strength nearly as much as spending hours in the weight room. It could refine your spin so that you have the fluid pedal stroke of a pro rider. It could boost your leg speed to track-sprinter proportions and endow you with enough power to stomp over steep hills. There would be a mountain biking bonus, too: You'd get a smooth, circular stroke that would help you maintain rear-wheel traction on rubble-strewn climbs.

Believe it or not, all this is possible if you simply unclip one foot and pedal with the other leg. Isolated leg training (ILT) forces you to turn smooth, powerful circles because the opposite leg doesn't help you through "dead spots" in the stroke (primarily when the pedal comes up and over the top). This forces your hip flexors and hamstrings to do much more work. Later, when you resume normal riding with both feet, your muscles will remember how to pedal correctly.

You can do ILT workouts indoors on a resistance trainer or outside using a road or mountain bike. Inside, just unclip one foot and rest it on a stool or chair, or reach back and hook it over the trainer. Some riders prop their free feet against their water bottle cages or, if they're flexible enough, put them up on the handlebar drops. Outside, let your un-clipped foot dangle just outside the arc of the pedal. Advanced riders can brace it against their chainstays, but be careful not to get caught in the whirling spokes. Use a hill with a steady, moderate grade to keep speed down and provide resistance. ILT isn't dangerous, but as with any training, it's best to avoid busy roads.

The Technique

With isolated leg training, you can work on strength or speed by varying resistance and cadence. At a slow 50 rpm, it's almost like weight training. Concentrate on different parts of the pedal stroke. Focus on pushing down for 50 revo-lutions, then on pulling up for 50. Work on a smooth transition across the bottom from downstroke to upstroke. A slower cadence helps you coordinate these movements better. You'll need to use the hip flexors on the front of your upper thigh to lift your leg. Because these mus-cles are weak in most riders, this training results in a faster, more efficient stroke. (To determine cadence, install a cyclecomputer with an rpm function or count pedal strokes for 15 seconds and multiply by four.)

When you're new to ILT, you'll notice right away that your one-leg pedal stroke is

Using one leg teaches you to claw the pedal through the bottom of the stroke.

lumpy or jerky. You may be afraid this will make your two-leg stroke equally inefficient, but the opposite is true. If you stick with ILT, you'll find that it eliminates the hole in your pedal circle.

Remember, ILT is primarily a strength exercise rather than a cardio-vascular workout. Your heart rate won't go up much when you're pedaling with one leg. Most riders don't even bother to check their heart-rate monitors when doing it.

The best thing about this training? You'll get fast results. The first time you try ILT, you'll have trouble pedaling even an easy gear for a minute or two. It will feel awkward and your muscles will tire quickly. It's a graphic illustration of just how inefficient your pedaling actually is. But after just three or four sessions, your stroke will get smoother and you'll be a stronger rider.

The following charts outline three workouts you can do inside or on the road. Do each workout three times. Be sure to get warm and loose with at least 20 minutes of easy two-leg pedaling. Gearing recommendations are approximate. Make adjustments if the ratios are too hard or easy. To make significant progress, do an ILT workout at least twice a week.

Workout 1

GEAR	CADENCE	WHAT TO DO
39×17T*	40–60	2 minutes with left leg
39×17T	40–60	2 minutes with right leg
39×17T	80–100	2 minutes of easy spinning with both legs
39×19T	80–90	2 minutes with left leg
39×19T	80–90	2 minutes with right leg
39×17T	80–100	2 minutes of easy spinning with both legs

*number of teeth on chainring × number of teeth on cog

Workout 2

GEAR	CADENCE	WHAT TO DO
53×15T	40–60	5 minutes with left leg
53×15T	40–60	5 minutes with right leg
39×17T	80–100	5 minutes of easy spinning with both legs

Workout 3

GEAR	CADENCE	WHAT TO DO
39×17T	80–100	3 minutes with left leg
39×17T	80–100	3 minutes with right leg
53×13T	40–60	3 minutes with both legs, pedaling hard
39×19T	80–100	3 minutes of easy spinning with both legs

9
Brain Training

Most people know the value of tools such as wrenches and screwdrivers. They help keep bikes running well. Like these tools, most of the techniques discussed in this book are easy to grasp and quickly useful. Others, though, are a little harder to get a handle on. One of the most important is the intangible called focus.

To be a successful cyclist, you need to set goals. Perhaps you're gearing up for a century ride or a big race, or maybe you just want to get over the next hill. Focus helps you reach these goals.

Focus can be described as narrowed attention. Focus is concentration. It lets you aim your vision and define your view. You choose a distant goal (usually a major event such as a tour, camp, or big ride you want to be in great shape for) and commit to preparing for it. Staying focused on the goal—sustaining a strong mental image of the event— makes it easier to put in the necessary work. It will get you out the door on rides that you may be tempted to skip.

Like the focusing power in the lens of a camera, mental focus lets you see things more clearly and concentrate on what's important. But unlike modern cameras, autofocus in your mind is not an option. You must develop this skill to key in on the right elements. Focus on a long-term goal is good, but don't forget about the short-term goals that get you there.

Here's an example. During preparation for the 1984 Olympics in Los Angeles, top U.S. cyclist Davis Phinney now admits to being so focused on his long-term goal that he lost the ability to enjoy riding in the short term. For almost 2 years before the Games, he was obsessed with competing, especially in the road race. "I created an image of the day in my mind so often that I was unable to think about or concentrate on much else," he says.

Phinney was adrift in a sea of Olympic hype, so much so that he was unable to appreciate his improvements and the races he won during that time. Looking back, he realizes, "My expectation was so high—winning was my only objective—that I set myself up for failure. I lost, finishing fifth in the road race and third in the team time trial."

Through that unhappy experience, Phinney learned that each step up the ladder should be savored and valued. Proper focus requires putting blinders on, but not so tightly that you miss what's right in front of you. You need to visualize not only your goal but also the process required to reach it. That's what creates successes along the way and prepares you for the ups, downs, and turns that you always encounter on the road to an ultimate objective. Phinney lacked this short-term focus, and that hurt his chances of winning a gold medal.

Zeroing In

Short-term focus is the ability to clear your mind of everything extraneous and concentrate on the task at hand. For example, work on your sprint for the race in 2 weeks instead of obsessing about the district championship in 6 weeks. Finish the last 5 miles of this 60-mile training ride instead of fretting about the century in September.

Successful short-term focus also means that at crucial moments you think only about cycling. "It's letting yourself be of the moment and in the moment, and no place else," as Phinney puts it.

Picture yourself riding in a group at a brisk pace, everyone close together. Every rider must keep a uniform speed and ride a straight line. This is no time to have your mind on the argument you just had with your spouse (probably about going on the ride) or the latest crisis at work. In the most intense moments of cycling, the likelihood of making a mistake increases if you don't have complete focus.

You may not even notice that your mind wanders at crucial times. On your next few rides, pay attention to how your mental state relates to various situations.

Studies have compared endurance athletes who zero in with those who zone out during events. Riders who focus on the task at hand (zero in) perform better. This is called association. The opposite, disassociation, is less productive because you take yourself out of the task rather than committing to it.

This isn't to say you must concentrate solely on cycling for every minute of every ride. It's natural to let your mind wander, and even beneficial in certain circumstances. Phinney's approach is to start each ride with a warmup period. "I let the clutter sort itself in my head before I concentrate purely on the ride itself." Let your thoughts ramble early, then clear your mind and focus on what you need to do on the bike. Phinney adds that the main reason he never rides with earphones—besides the fact that it's dangerous to not be able to hear traffic—is because music is a distraction.

In racing, the ability to totally focus is essential. It can make all the difference. "My best cycling moments," Phinney says, "are those times when my head is completely clear and all I'm doing is processing information, right as it happens, right at that instant. This is critical—especially in the final 200 meters if you are a sprinter like I was."

As Phinney discovered, learning to focus will certainly improve performance. But there's another benefit to acquiring this tool. Think about the principle in less-competitive terms. You power eat through lunch while reading the paper, and the stereo is on and the kids are running around the kitchen. As you put the plate in the sink, you realize you didn't even taste the food because of all the distractions. Then you spoon out some ice cream you've been craving. As you start to eat, all else is forgotten and the sweet taste becomes your focus. It's the most delicious bowl of ice cream you've ever had. You savor every bite.

Now, don't focus on ice cream every day. This example is simply to point out that the more concentrated your focus is, the more concentrated your pleasure is. This is certainly true in cycling. You may find that the time you feel most alive is during and right after a period of absolute focus. To train yourself to concentrate and reach this point, do what can be termed mental intervals. Focus on your breathing for 1 minute, then focus on your pedaling for 1 minute. Back and forth. As with any interval workout, rest between these periods.

The Grin Factor

As Phinney trained himself to concentrate, his race results improved. Then an unexpected bonus began following especially intense finishes, when a smile would instantly crease his face and a feeling of exhilaration would wash over him. He began calling this the grin factor.

The grin factor turns out to be an accurate gauge of how much fun something is. Think of ripping down a fast descent, going faster than you previously dared, on the edge but in control. At the bottom, you punch a fist in the air and let out a whoop. Or, you're spinning along in a paceline where everyone is riding in sync and the miles just fly by. When the group pulls in at the customary water stop, everyone beams and starts talking at once.

Sometimes, the feeling is more subtle. Maybe you're rolling along by yourself on a road you've ridden many times, but on this ride you notice everything and it's special: the color of the sky, the softness of the air, the hum of your tires on the pavement.

"With my competitive days behind me, the grin factor has become even more important," Phinney says. "It's what I love about cycling, and focus is what makes it happen."

10
Avoiding No-Man's-Land

In the savage battles of World War I, the ravaged ground between entrenched armies was called no-man's-land. Cordoned off by barbed wire and bombardment, it was a fierce obstacle to victory. In the fight for greater fitness, no-man's-land is a metaphor used by cycling coach Tom Ehrhard to describe the unproductive heart-rate training zone many riders get trapped in. Here's how it works.

You need low-intensity/long-duration training to build what Ehrhard calls an aerobic infrastructure. But if you always train at low heart rates, you develop endurance with no top-end speed. You get sawed off in races or group rides when the pace quickens. Your goal of riding a faster century never gets realized.

"If you want to be competitive, you have to develop your max VO_2 (maximal oxygen consumption) with occasional hard efforts," says Dean Golich, a cycling coach in Colorado Springs. Conversely, if you train hard most of the time, you never recover. Chronic fatigue will result in overtraining and poison your performance.

The solution is obvious. You need to mix hard training with plenty of easy pedaling for recovery. But this is a lot simpler to say than it is for most riders to practice. Think about what happens on a typical ride. You start easily, but as you warm up, your speed increases until you settle into a semi-hard pace. For the rest of the ride, you're cranking along, breathing quickly but not gasping. It's a satisfying level of work because it feels pretty hard yet it's not too painful to maintain. You must be getting lots of benefit from this, right?

Wrong. This is exactly the wrong zone to train in, particularly if you are a rider with some experience who is advancing in the sport. You're going too hard to recover but too easy to crank up your max VO_2. You're riding in no-man's-land.

Recipe for Mediocrity

"Training in the middle, going moderately hard, makes you tired, so you can't do enough volume at lower levels or enough intensity at higher heart rates to really improve," says Golich.

Ehrhard agrees. "NML (no-man's-land) workouts provide a kinesthetic sense of 'working hard,' but they expose the rider to too much stress per unit of gain."

Real improvement requires discipline on both ends of the intensity spectrum. But Ehrhard notes, "Many riders I coach come back after their first recovery ride and say it was way too easy. The same riders tell me their interval workouts are too hard." So they confine themselves to no-man's-land—and mediocrity.

As an example, assume that a typical rider has a maximum heart rate of 180 beats per minute (bpm). According to the training zones recommended by Golich, this rider would do easy recovery rides at up to 65 percent of maximum. That's 117 bpm. Basic aerobic work is 66 to 72 percent of max, or 119 to 130 bpm. Harder aerobic riding is 73 to 80 percent, or 131 to 144 bpm. Intervals and max-VO_2 workouts jump to 85 to 90 percent, a heart rate of 153 to 162.

Notice the gap between 80 and 85 percent. That's no-man's-land, sandwiched between the top of the aerobic zone and the bottom of the interval zone. Cyclists are tempted to ride there because it feels like a hard workout but it doesn't make them suffer miserably. Therein lies the danger.

The Great Escape

Daily NML efforts create a mild but long-lasting fatigue. You get more aerobic improvement from riding at lower heart rates because you can do more and recover faster. At the same time, there's too little work for real top-end improvement. Fortunately, dodging no-man's-land is simple. If you do it correctly, says Ehrhard, "riding easy will seem too easy and riding hard will seem too hard."

Spend much of your training time in the low-intensity recovery, basic aerobic, and harder aerobic training zones. This promotes an aerobic base but doesn't cost much in terms of stress and glycogen depletion. These rides should be "guilt-producingly slow," says Skip Hamilton, a masters champion and a national-class endurance athlete who frequently coaches at cycling camps in the Rocky Mountains.

Then when you train hard, train really hard. Intensity must be near or above your lactate threshold (85 percent to more than 90 percent of maximum heart rate). Such training "will seem extremely difficult, mentally," warns Ehrhard. "It's why many racers only do this level of effort in competition, hence the phrase 'racing into form.' The secret is to use a heart-rate monitor to establish the correct training intensity, rather than go by how you feel."

What if you're aiming for an event, such as a fast century, where experience has shown that the forbidden 80 to 85 percent of max heart rate is your optimum intensity for the distance? No problem. "Training above and below no-man's-land automatically extends your abilities in that range, too," says Ehrhard.

A Different View

Arnie Baker, M.D., a top masters competitor who is a member of *Bicycling* magazine's Fitness Advisory Board and author of *Smart Cycling*, acknowledges the existence of no-man's-land (he calls it the no zone), but he says it's dangerous territory only for advanced riders. For cycling newcomers or riders who are still developing basic fitness, he has this advice: Go there.

For a very fit rider, Dr. Baker explains, 85 percent of maximum heart rate is the upper limit of aerobic capacity. It means working hard but not going all-out. But for a lower-level rider, 85 percent of max is much more intense. In fact, the 80 to 85 percent range defines a time-trial effort for most intermediate cyclists. In Dr. Baker's view, "Training in this range is as vital for beginning racers and fast recreational riders as the 90-plus percent zone is for seasoned racers. The perceived effort and effects on the body are the same."

Dr. Baker recommends that most rides be done at a hard pace if you have limited time to train. "Recovery will occur on days when you aren't riding at all," he says. "In most cases, expanding your cruising speed by frequently training at 80 to 85 percent of max is crucial."

Another reason to train at this level, Dr. Baker says, is because that's where you'll find yourself during a fast century and most group training rides.

If you cannot ride well at an exertion level of 80 to 85 percent, you can also expect to struggle against headwinds and on long climbs, Dr. Baker warns. In his opinion, only if you have no difficulties in these situations or when you are riding in a fast group does it makes sense to avoid training in no-man's-land.

PART THREE

Coaches' Approaches

11
Best Tips from Top Coaches

Cycling coaches have traditionally been a secretive lot. When they found a method that worked, they often didn't share their insights with others. Only a select few riders would ever benefit from even the best coach's knowledge.

This changed in the mid-1990s as the U.S. Cycling Team launched Project 96 to prepare riders for the Atlanta Olympics. Heading the effort were Chris Carmichael, who was then the national coaching director, and Ed Burke, Ph.D., cycling physiologist and director of the exercise-science program at the University of Colorado at Colorado Springs, who served as coordinator. Project 96 sought to pool information and develop technology and training methods that would help U.S. cyclists perform well at the Games.

One of the best results of Project 96 was the Solidarity Coaching Conference held at the Olympic Training Center (OTC) in Colorado Springs. This was the biggest gathering of cycling brainpower ever assembled. Cycling coaches, physicians, and sports scientists from Italy, Spain, Germany, Canada, and the United States met to exchange their findings.

Here are the best tips, techniques, and training advice from the world's top cycling minds who were at that conference.

Massimo Testa, M.D.

Dr. Testa is a pro cycling team physician who has planned training for riders including former world champion and Olympian Lance Armstrong. He is internationally respected for defining the optimum combination of work and rest that pro riders need to maintain form through their grueling 9-month racing season.

Get plenty of rest year-round. "I used to prescribe lots of intensity, but maybe the riders were overtrained," said Dr. Testa. "Now, I schedule more rest days along with several easy weeks during the season. Top European pro Adriano Baffi trained only every other day in 1994 and he had his best season. We watch carefully for signs of overtraining, including decreased power and speed; increased recovery time; tactical mistakes including dumb crashes; digestive trouble; weight loss; anx-

41

iety; depression; and a bad attitude. If these signs appear, we modify training.

"Recreational riders can do the same. If you crash or get sick or have bad psychology, you have to take some time off."

Work on strength and flexibility, too. "We try to prevent problems by doing abdominal exercises and stretching," Dr. Testa said. "A study has shown that cyclists increase their power by 5 percent merely by stretching the hamstrings, because added flexibility means better utilization of the quadriceps. We also change their position on the bike if it's needed. But we never adjust their position during the race season even if it's bad because they wouldn't have time to adjust and might get injured.

"In the off-season, we use rollers three to five times a week to improve balance and spin. And we do weight training to restore muscle mass lost during the season. Studies show that Tour de France riders gain body fat during the race because they lose muscle volume, especially in the upper body. Winter is the time to counter that effect. We do three sets of 25 reps at 50 percent of the maximum they can lift in that exercise, followed by two sets of 50 reps at 25 percent of max weight. We use high reps and low weights because when you pedal, you use a small percentage of maximum strength on each stroke. We also ride some climbs of 4 to 6 minutes, pedaling at 50 to 60 rpm to build strength and muscle mass."

Tudor Bompa, Ph.D.

Often called the father of periodization training, Dr. Bompa is a legendary figure among endurance coaches. His theories were the basis for East German and Soviet success in the 1980s, and he advocated weight training for endurance athletes before it became widely accepted. He is a professor at York University in Toronto.

Plan to meet your goals, but don't be rigid. "Training regimens must be flexible," according to Dr. Bompa. "You have to plan for the total stress load in your life, not just the stress from training. Total stress includes job, family, school. You can't divorce training from other aspects of your life."

Watch out for too much intensity. "You only improve if you overload your system with occasional hard training. But overloading often leads to overtraining. If you regenerate with easy rides and rest, you'll super-compensate and be better. Don't think 'hard work.' Instead, think 'intelligent work.' Most North Americans are overtrained. When you're ready, you'll feel good physically and mentally. That's when you should do the big event."

Repeat workouts to get a training effect. "If you want to develop endurance for a century ride, start doing a long weekend ride at least one month before the event."

After a hard session, set aside 30 minutes to regenerate. "Sip a carb replacement drink; lie down with your legs elevated; relax mentally, maybe take a 15-minute nap. Even if you have to borrow the time from training, you'll recover much faster."

Heavy weights deserve another look. "I've seen some preliminary results on a track pursuiter who weighed 154 pounds and shifted to power lifting for 2 years. Then he could squat with more than 500 pounds. When he returned to the bike, his pursuit time decreased by 5 seconds. Although we cannot draw universal conclusions, this example is fascinating."

Chris Carmichael

Carmichael rode professionally with the pioneering 7-Eleven team that launched U.S. cycling into the big time. Later, his vision and drive turned the OTC into a worldwide leader in training techniques. Still Lance Armstrong's personal coach, Carmichael combines the ability to set broad seasonal goals with minutely planned daily training.

Create a vision statement and set goals. "This is important whether you're an elite rider or preparing to ride your first century," said Carmichael. "A vision statement shouldn't be a bunch of touchy-feely stuff. It's designed to provide a long-term goal and direct your actions and emotions. Before you write it, ask yourself, 'If I were to drop dead tomorrow, what would I want people to say about me?' Then write it down. That's your vision statement.

"For instance, here's the U.S. pro riders' group vision statement: 'One hundred percent prepared physically and mentally to race to the full potential of the entire team.' Then they formulated four goals that would help them achieve that. One, a united and committed team. Two, an organized training plan. Three, a clear and defined race strategy. Four, maintain control and commitment to the vision during unplanned disruptions.

"With these as guidelines, you should be able to set up your own vision and goals. For instance, number four is a great goal for every recreational rider who has to deal with a job and family."

Dean Golich

Golich, a cycling coach in Colorado Springs, made his mark with hard work and careful attention to detail. As the recorder and analyzer of the day-to-day training and exercise intensities of national-team riders, he accumulated a wealth of on-bike information. His secret weapon? He's a strong cyclist himself and was able to keep up with the team on most of their training rides to monitor their performances.

Ride the machine. "The following ergometer test, devised by the OTC sports-science and -technology division, is a quick way to track your fitness from one month to the next or compare your power to other riders," said Golich. "We often use it to screen riders. You need an ergometer that measures power output in watts. Check at a health club or university human-performance lab. The CompuTrainer, which we use at the OTC, has this feature. If you aren't interested in comparing yourself to others, you can use a resistance trainer and simply increase your gears instead of the watts. After a good warmup, do the following progression."

0 to 3 minutes at 110 watts
3 to 6 minutes at 180 watts
6 to 9 minutes at 250 watts
9 to 12 minutes at 340 watts
12 to 15 minutes at 410 watts
15 to 18 minutes at 480 watts

"These figures are for a 6-foot, 155-pound rider. If you are larger or smaller, increase or decrease watts proportionally. Keep your cadence at 90 rpm. When it falls below 90 for more than 10 seconds, the test is over. This is an all-out test, so check with your doctor before attempting it.

"Elite national-class male riders usually score over 15 minutes for seniors and over 13 for juniors. Women are generally 15 to 20 percent lower. In a similar test, former Olympic champion and pro racer Olaf Ludwig pounded out 600 watts."

Make full use of race data. "If you have a heart-rate monitor that stores information for downloading, wear it during a race or competi-

tive ride. Then compare your maximum heart rate and other information with the data collected during training. Most of our riders find that
in competition they can reach a higher heart rate and time trial for extended periods at a higher heart rate than they can in training. When we
know that, we can reset their training zones. For instance, when Lance
Armstrong is racing in Europe, he faxes us his heart-rate profile from
races. We can suggest how hard he should train the next week."

Know your body. "People say that an elevated morning heart rate
means you're overtrained. This is a good indicator for some riders. But
I've seen other riders have their best races when their heart rates were 10
percent higher than normal."

Ed Burke, Ph.D.

Instrumental in America's Olympic cycling success since 1984, Dr.
Burke has written prolifically about cycling science for two decades.
Much of his research over the years has been in nutrition and hydration—subjects that are crucial in the heat and humidity of the summer
cycling season.

Determine your unique maximum heart rate. "Most training plans
are based on maximum heart rate, so you need an accurate figure," said
Dr. Burke. "Here's how to get it: Warm up thoroughly, then on a long,
consistent hill with little traffic, steadily increase effort every minute for
about 10 minutes until you can't go any faster. Then sprint. If possible,
use a recording heart-rate monitor so you don't have to think about
numbers when you're working at your max. Don't do this test unless
you are rested and have fresh legs. Stay hydrated because heart rate rises
when you're dehydrated, even though power output remains the same.
Also, get permission from your doctor before you try this test."

Pack in carb right after riding. "In a study, two groups of cyclists
were exercised to exhaustion. One group drank a carbohydrate replacement drink immediately after exercise, and the other group waited 2
hours. Analysis of muscle tissue showed that the riders who reloaded
immediately after the workout produced muscle glycogen at a rate 50
percent higher than the group that waited."

Get enough carb. "Most cyclists who train hard need 8 to 10 grams
of carbohydrate per kilogram (2.2 pounds) of body weight to replenish
their glycogen stores. A banana contains 40 grams, and a bagel, 50.
Check the labels on packaged foods to help calculate your intake."

Switch on your metabolism. "Research conducted by John Ivy, Ph.D., at the University of Texas in Austin, shows that including some protein in carbohydrate drinks turns on a metabolic switch that increases insulin secretion and stimulates uptake of both protein and carbohydrate in muscle cells. Such drinks are known commercially as metabolic optimizers and can be found at health food stores and some bike shops." Not only are the drinks a good postride supplement but some riders are also having success after drinking them during long events.

Hennie Top

A leading Dutch racer in the early 1980s, Top served as U.S. national women's road coach in the 1990s. She is respected as a master of tactics and strategy.

Climb at your own pace. "Don't let others dictate your effort. If you aren't a good climber, try to start a long climb at the front of the group and slide gradually to the back as the climb progresses. Maybe you can hang on over the top. Even when you are riding alone, don't go so hard that you blow up halfway up the hill. You won't be able to recover on the descent."

If you lose time on climbs, make it up on descents. "Follow an experienced rider down the hill, but don't follow too closely, in case she makes a mistake and crashes. Also, keep your legs going around so they don't stiffen up for the next climb."

Jeff Broker, Ph.D.

Broker, chief biomechanist with the U.S. Olympic Committee, is an expert on pedaling mechanics. He pioneered the use of the SRM Power-Meter in the United States. This German device allows a cyclist's power output to be measured on the bike in actual riding conditions and is instrumental in calculating aerodynamic drag forces for time trialists.

Better aerodynamics save more time than better pedaling. "It's a myth that riders pull up at the bottom of the pedal stroke sufficiently to unload the pedal," Dr. Broker stated. "There's also no scientific evidence that improved pedaling mechanics can shave seconds off your time. In fact, lower-level cyclists often have better form than elite riders. And our studies show that mountain bikers seem to pull through at the bottom of the pedal stroke better than track or road riders. Maybe it's because mountain bikers need uniform power delivery through the whole pedal stroke so they don't lose traction on loose surfaces. Theoretically, better pedaling techniques should make you a better cyclist, but scientifically it doesn't seem to be that important.

"Aerodynamics will make you faster than perfect pedaling style. Here's a great example. Wind tunnel results show that eliminating 10 grams of drag saves 158 feet in a 25-mile time trial. How much is 10 grams? It's the drag created by projecting about 4 inches of a pencil into the air stream. That baggy jersey or upright riding position is costing you minutes."

Nicholas Torrados, M.D., Ph.D.

As physician for ONCE, one of Europe's top pro teams, Dr. Torrados was known as an expert in altitude training. ONCE (pronounced "own-say") pioneered scientific training for pro riders, and Dr. Torrados took a mobile lab to every race so that he could monitor cyclists throughout the season.

Hike before you bike. "Early-season training for the ONCE team includes 1 hour of walking in the morning before training on the bike," according to Dr. Torrados. "We also do some uphill running. This helps condition the legs for the intense cycling training during the season. It isn't traditional for cyclists to hike and run, but we think it's important. We even do our first performance test of the season running on the treadmill."

Determine your lactate threshold (LT). "Most cyclists don't have access to lab facilities to determine their lactate thresholds. But you can find yours with a 30-minute time trial. The average heart rate you can maintain for this ride—about 10 miles—is a good working approximation of your lactate threshold." Training at intensities from 10 percent below LT to slightly above it will improve your time trialing and overall cycling efficiency.

Wolfram Lindner

As national-team road coach for the former East Germany, Lindner created one of the world's most powerful amateur cycling squads. At the time of the coaching conference, he was in charge of the Swiss national team. Although Lindner is dictatorial and uncompromising in his beliefs, his ready wit enlivened his address.

Don't concentrate too much on improving weaknesses. "We work extensively on riders' strengths and also try to improve their weaknesses," said Lindner. "But never spend so much time on your weaknesses that you lose your strengths. For instance, we had a great sprinter who suffered with the fourth group on climbs. He worked on climbing all winter, and when racing began, he could climb with the third group. But he could no longer sprint well."

Rest as hard as you train. "Olaf Ludwig rode 26,000 miles in the 12 months before his Olympic victory in 1988. But when you train as intensely as we did, you have to rest just as hard. We went to Mexico for 6 weeks of altitude training, and when we got back, my boss in East Germany looked at all the rest days and said we could have saved money by only staying 4 weeks. He didn't understand the need for rest."

Roy Knickman

A product of the "class of '84" that included Olympic road champion Alexi Grewal and future pro stars Ron Kiefel and Davis Phinney, Knickman also raced professionally before taking over as U.S. national-team road coach. His advice served as a refreshingly simple closer to the coaching conference.

Don't calculate potential success based on test scores. "When I was 15, I had a max VO_2 (maximal oxygen consumption) of 72 and was viewed as the next great American rider. Each year after that, my VO_2 numbers decreased even though my results got better. Right after my bronze-medal performance in the 1984 Olympic-team time trial—the strongest I've ever been—I was tested again. My max VO_2 was 64."

12
Go Fast

Ever dreamed of following the wheel of a pro-cycling veteran, soaking up techniques as you ride? Or having a team physician suggest how to train and eat? Each season, this is a reality at cycling camps throughout the country. Some are geared toward road riders, others are for mountain bikers, and there are even camps exclusively for women. There's no better way for an enthusiastic rider to spend a week. Total immersion at a camp results in an all-around education that produces fitness, confidence, and the springboard for long-term improvement.

This was reality recently for 45 riders at the Go Fast! camp conducted by former Olympic cyclists Connie Carpenter and Davis Phinney in Beaver Creek, Colorado. For 5 days, the campers rode tight pacelines, practiced sprints and cornering, and climbed high mountain passes. Here is some of what those riders experienced.

As husband and wife, Phinney and Carpenter are the First Couple of U.S. cycling. Connie won the first-ever Olympic road race for women in 1984, and Davis won more than 300 races in his historic career, including two stages of the Tour de France. They do business as Carpenter/Phinney Cycling Camps with the assistance of a staff of cycling luminaries. In addition to Connie and Davis, riders at Go Fast! got to hear from and pedal with experts Massimo Testa, M.D., pro cycling team physician; Andrew Pruitt, Ed.D., cycling's foremost physical therapist; John Teaford, speed skater and track cyclist; Ed Burke, Ph.D., cycling physiologist and director of the exercise-science program at the University of Colorado at Colorado Springs; Skip Hamilton, masters champion and national-class endurance athlete who frequently coaches at cycling camps in the Rocky Mountains; Ray Browning, top Ironman distance triathlete and cyclist; and Ron Kiefel, longtime U.S. pro road racer and Olympic medalist.

How Pros Train, by Massimo Testa, M.D.

Training has changed radically. Fifteen years ago, cyclists took 2 months off after the season, trained easily in winter, then raced into shape. Now, riders take only 2 weeks of easy riding as a break and have 8,000 miles in their legs before the first race in February. Also, slow endurance rides have been abandoned. Back in the 1960s and 1970s, Eddy Merckx, the world's best racer, used to ride across Belgium at an easy pace—a 9-hour ride—then sleep on a train coming back. Then he'd do it again the next day. But now, even long training rides are done at only 25 beats per minute below lactate threshold (LT).

Weight training is necessary to develop strength and power, because riders are going at speeds unimaginable 10 years ago. Top sprinters can use a 54×11-tooth gear and reach 45 mph. It's like they're on motorcycles. So we use light weights—about half of the one-rep maximum in a given exercise—and do as many as 50 or 60 reps with short rests between sets. In winter, we often do an hour on the rollers in the morning, lift weights at noon, and cross-country ski before dinner.

We spend a lot of time building LT, which is the level of intensity at which your body can just handle the lactic acid building up. You can approximate your LT by determining your average heart rate for a 10-mile time trial. If you then train extensively at two or three beats below this figure, you'll see big improvements. For instance, one of the top riders of the early 1980s, Italy's Giuseppe Saronni, pushed 425 watts at his LT. Former world champion and Olympian Lance Armstrong, with the same max VO_2 (maximal oxygen consumption), pushes more than 500. The difference? Lance does a lot of training near his LT.

Keep a training diary and record your resting morning heart rate and weight. Check heart rate twice a week—the morning before hard training and again 2 days later. If heart rate is elevated five beats above normal, you're in danger of overtraining, and need to rest. Check your weight to spot glycogen depletion. Average-size riders usually carry 1 to 2 pounds of glycogen in their muscles, so if they're down in weight, it isn't a good day to train near their LTs. But it's fine to ride long and easy—up to 65 percent of max heart rate—to train the body to use fat for fuel.

Sweat that smells like ammonia is a sign you are overtrained and glycogen-depleted, and that you're destroying muscle as you ride. It indicates catabolism and means you aren't respecting your need for rest.

To improve your wattage output by 20 percent, ride up a moderate hill in a 53×15T gear at 40 to 60 rpm. Do 5 to 15 repeats of 40 to 120 seconds each in three sets. Recover for twice the time you push hard. Don't do this workout more than twice a week or if you have knee trouble. Be well-rested, and be sure to warm up thoroughly.

Quicker Cornering, by Davis Phinney

When I went to Europe to race, I thought I knew how to corner. One day, we were hurtling down this wicked descent in France and I was trying to catch the group ahead. I was flying. Suddenly, I realized I had caught up so fast because the next corner was a U-turn and they'd slowed way down. I got partway around, locked up the brakes, and went catapulting over a stone wall into a vineyard. It took 5 minutes to find my bike. After that, I decided I'd better think through this cornering business. It's as important as actual physical training for maximizing speed. Here's the technique I learned.

Start the turn by putting the outside pedal down and weighting it hard (see photo). Push it down like you want to break it off. Lean the bike into the corner by countersteering—pushing down on the handlebar with your inside hand. Have your butt on the rear of the saddle and stay low along the top tube. Don't lean your upper body into the turn. Instead, let the bike lean underneath you. When you countersteer, you don't need to push the inside handlebar forward like you would on a heavy motorcycle. Just push down on the inside bar.

The key move is to rotate your inside hip forward so that your inside knee goes against the top tube instead of pointing into the turn. This twist causes the outside of your pelvis to push the seat over, immediately angling the bike into the turn. (Remember my rule number one: Lean the bike and it will turn.) Your inside arm naturally straightens because you are twisting your upper body away from the turn. You are allowing the bike to fall over as far as it needs to. Doing it this way, you can fly through a series of sharp corners with a tight line, quickly shifting the bike side to side under you. The hip-twist motion is the key.

If you are a downhill skier, think of how you turn on snow. You weight the outside ski, push it into the hill, angulate in at the knee and

Ex-pro Ron Kiefel shows how to turn by leaning the bike, not the body.

hips, and keep your upper body upright. You turn from the feet, not from the shoulders. It works the same on a bike.

Other tips for cornering:

■ Set up a line of paper cups in an empty parking lot and practice this cornering technique at least once a week. Weave around the cups, making left and right turns back and forth. Do this even if you aren't racing, because you never know when you'll need this skill in traffic or to dodge a dog running out at you.

■ This technique makes it easy to change your line partway through a turn. If you suddenly see gravel or an oil patch, just let the bike become a little more vertical. This will straighten your arc until you're past the danger, then you can push the inside bar down again to complete the turn.

■ In successive turns, use the current one to set up the next one. Approach wide, cut the apex, then quickly shift the bike under you to set up the next corner.

Better Bike Fit, by Andrew Pruitt, Ed.D.

Always remember: Adjust the bike to fit your body. Don't try to make your body fit the bike. My favorite way to say this is, "The bike should look like you." For instance, if you have one long arm, don't hesitate to upset symmetry by moving the brake lever farther down the handlebar on that side. Do what's necessary to accommodate your body and achieve a comfortable, balanced fit.

If you can't touch your toes with your knees straight and no warmup, you'll have trouble achieving a modern aerodynamic riding position. The remedy is a 15-minute routine of daily stretching.

A leg-length discrepancy of only 4 to 6 millimeters can become a problem when combined with clipless pedals. With old-fashioned slotted cleats, the foot on the short leg could rise slightly at the bottom of the pedal stroke to compensate. With clipless pedals, it can't. The solution is to place a shim under the cleat of the shorter leg.

Chronic saddle sores on one side of your crotch indicate a bad fit. They usually mean that you are sitting crooked in the saddle. Suspect a leg-length discrepancy.

If you want to achieve the most effective time-trial position using an aero handlebar, you have two choices. You can position the elbow rests wide so the air flows between your arms and around your chest. Or you can move the rests close together so your arms cut the air like a ship's prow. To determine which position works best for you, time yourself while coasting down a long, steady hill in calm conditions.

Our work with national-team riders has found that body width on the bike is more important than height on the bike. So work on making yourself narrow, but don't worry about how tall this may make you sit. For proof, recall Miguel Indurain. This five-time Tour de France winner was among the sport's best time trialists, but he sat noticeably more upright than most of his competitors.

Paceline Pointers, by John Teaford

When you reach the front of the line, keep the pace steady. Check your cyclecomputer and maintain the speed of the person who had been leading (assuming there's no change in terrain or wind direction). You take the front because the former leader pulls over and slows slightly, not because you accelerate.

If you are dropping back to the rear of the paceline after your turn at the front and a gap opens between you and the last rider, your only purpose in life should be to get back on. It's easier to stay with the group than to push all that air by yourself.

Stay off the brakes by looking ahead and recognizing things that will change the paceline's speed. Drift slightly to the side to catch more wind if you are running up on someone's rear wheel. If you need your brakes, ease them on with one finger as you soft pedal. Don't make any abrupt changes in speed that disrupt rhythm and put everyone behind you in danger.

If your arms are tense and you get bumped from the side, the shock will go directly to the front wheel and cause you to swerve. Keep your elbows bent and relaxed to absorb contact so your steering isn't affected.

Heart Monitoring, by Ed Burke, Ph.D.

Using a heart-rate monitor is essential for anyone who is serious about performance. A monitor helps us develop our fitness and understand what our bodies are doing. There's a big difference between how we think we feel and how we really are. The heart monitor tells us how we really are.

Some riders have begun using the Karvonnen, or "heart-rate reserve," method to calculate their heart-rate training zones. The result may be closer to max-VO_2 values than the standard method. Here's how it's done.

1. Find your maximum heart rate in a lab or by steadily increasing your effort on a long hill until you can't drive it any higher. (Always get your doctor's approval before undertaking such strenuous exertion.)

2. Subtract your resting heart rate from your maximum heart rate.

3. Calculate 65, 75, 80, and 90 percent of the resulting number.

4. Add your resting heart rate to each value to get your four exercise levels. Use these when applying a training program based on heart-rate zones.

If your perceived exertion is high but heart rate is low, it's a red flag. You are probably overtrained, dehydrated, or chronically glycogen-depleted. Examine your training plan and diet, and make corrections.

Stay hydrated to ensure accuracy during heart-rate training. Sweat comes from plasma, the watery part of the blood. So as you become dehydrated, your blood volume shrinks, and your heart has to pump faster to compensate. This is called cardiac drift. It means you aren't getting as much training benefit from a given heart rate as you would when adequately hydrated.

Foods and Fluids, by Skip Hamilton

Don't forget to use your "glycogen window." The more carbohydrate you consume in the hour or so after riding, the better glycogen stores are replenished. This is why you see pro-team coaches rush to their riders after a race and hand them bottles of energy drink. This won't just help you recover for your next training session, you'll feel better at work or school the next day, too.

A little protein and fat along with your preride carbohydrate foods seems to extend the effects of the carbs. Don't get carried away by the fat-free mania. Many good cyclists eat a couple of eggs with their pancakes before a long training ride or century. In fact, some cyclists are going back to lean red meat in the belief that it helps them recover from hard training.

For long rides away from fluid sources, fill a backpack-style hydration system with water and put a concentrated energy drink in your bottles. Mix it twice as strong as the directions say. Then dilute the drink to its proper concentration in your stomach by chasing each swig with water.

If you're training hard, have high-octane, nutritional snacks handy at work or around the house. This way, you won't be a victim of the vending machine. Try fruits, fig bars, bagels, graham crackers, and energy bars. Eat five or more small meals each day rather than three big ones, so your body has a constant supply of energy instead of a series of full/empty intervals.

If you aren't getting up at least once during the night to urinate, you are probably dehydrated. Carry a water bottle with you all day and keep nipping at it.

Mental Fitness, by Ray Browning

In my opinion, the mental aspects of performance are the most neglected yet most powerful influence on how we ride. These are my four keys to mental fitness.

1. Self-talk. What we say to ourselves has a huge impact on how we perform. Come up with a positive affirmation such as "Yes!" or "Feeling strong!" and use it when your motivation is low. On the other hand, don't try to talk yourself through a bout of overtraining. Self-talk won't help if your body is desperately crying for rest.

2. Imagery. We can create a mental image of what we want to achieve. Take 5 minutes to relax and picture yourself climbing strongly, breathing hard but in control, pedaling powerfully. Then when you are actually climbing, pull that image out of the mental file so it becomes reality. Remember that top performance isn't comfortable, so when you build your image of an event, be sure to include the appropriate strain and pain.

3. Focus. Elite performers think about breathing, technique, and the event itself. They think about how they can go faster right now. Non-elite riders go slower because they tend to disassociate. They think

about work or they go through elaborate mental processes to forget the discomfort—like designing houses in their heads, from the ground up. What do you think about on a 2-hour ride? Work? Relationships? Or are you thinking about how to improve your pedal stroke, your breathing, your cornering, your climbing?

4. Relaxation. Check your shoulders while you ride. Are they hunched up against your neck? Is your face relaxed? Tight muscles waste enormous amounts of energy. Your ability to relax is enhanced if you are comfortable with your abilities. For instance, you'll be relaxed in corners if you've taken the time to practice the cornering technique that Davis has described.

Here's a favorite tip: When intensity increases, concentrate on what it feels like, not on what it means. Focus on heart rate, breathing, the feeling in your legs. Don't think about how close you are to your anaerobic threshold and how soon you'll blow up if the pace stays high.

Yearly Plan, by Connie Carpenter

I used to be a speed skater. Back then, when my Norwegian coach gave me a training schedule, I followed it like a recipe for banana bread—put in exact amounts of this and that ingredient, and it will come out just so. Nowadays, I don't measure anything when I cook. I put ingredients in the batter, taste it, and make changes. That's how training should work, too. Take the list of ingredients and vary the recipe. The results will taste a little different for each cyclist.

Set goals so you know how a given training week fits into the big picture of the whole year—or even the rest of your life. You can't control the weather or your inherited talent or maybe even your work schedule. But you can control the thoughtful progression toward your goals. So get a big wall calendar with the whole year on it. Pencil in your goals and a general idea of what you want to do each day to reach them.

The biggest mistake most riders make is to ride the same pace all the time. Vary your speed. Do some sprints, then pedal slowly, then do a 5-minute jam. Don't get stuck in a rut.

Ten hours a week for training is a magical number for most riders. If you can train this much during each 7-day period, you can achieve most of your genetic potential. You'll have time to go hard but also to take some easy days. If you're pressed for time on certain days, try doing two short rides. Go hard for an hour in the morning, then pedal easily after work to help you recover faster.

Pro Workouts, by Ron Kiefel

First, find a good group to ride with. This is key to staying motivated and making yourself train at the proper intensities. I've been fortunate to have terrific guys to ride with over the years. We can ride hard and work together, or we can just pedal along. We don't have to be competitive on every ride.

Here's a sample training week containing two great workouts for boosting your lactate threshold (LT). These rides will improve your century performance or time trialing and make you a better all-around rider. Be sure you have a base of at least 6 weeks of aerobic riding at 60 to 80 percent of max heart rate before you use this schedule. Then divide your training into 4-week cycles. Work hard for 3 weeks, then go back to easy aerobic rides in the fourth week to recover.

Sunday: Take a long endurance ride at 65 to 85 percent of max heart rate.

Monday: Take a recovery ride for 1 hour, going easy at 60 to 75 percent of max heart rate.

Tuesday: Do an LT ladder on a long hill. After a 20-minute warmup, ride 2 minutes at a heart rate that's within five beats of your lactate threshold. Recover for 1 minute at 60 percent of max heart rate. Then do 4 minutes at LT, recover 2 minutes; 6 minutes at LT, recover 2 minutes; 8 minutes at LT, recover 2 minutes; 6 minutes at LT, recover 6 minutes; 4 minutes at LT, recover 2 minutes; 2 minutes at LT, recover 1 minute. You can recover while still going uphill by "walking" the bike in your lowest gear, or you can turn around and pedal slowly as you coast down.

Wednesday: Repeat Monday's recovery ride.

Thursday: Do continuous LT training on rolling terrain. Elevate your heart rate to within five beats of LT for one to three bouts of 10 to 20 minutes. This is great for teaching you how to apportion your energy and use gears that keep your legs spinning and supple.

Friday: Rest.

Saturday: Repeat Monday's recovery ride.

Occasionally, do the following workout to improve your lactate tolerance, substituting it for the hard training on Tuesday or Thursday. Go 2
to 3 minutes at up to 95 percent of your LT, then recover for 60 seconds
by spinning an easy gear. Work up to three sets of three repeats.

13
Zoning In

Joe Friel is a masters racer and cycling coach who has written one of
the most respected books for serious riders, *The Cyclist's Training Bible*.
His approach to workouts is a bit different in that he bases training
zones not on percentages of maximum heart rate but on percentages of
lactate-threshold heart rate (LTHR). One advantage is that it's less
stressful to determine LTHR than max heart rate. The resulting training
zones, however, are actually very close to those already described in this
book. Note that Friel does not subscribe to the no-man's-land concept
discussed in chapter 10.

Because the program uses heart rate to determine workout intensity,
you need a reliable wireless heart-rate monitor, ideally one that calcu-
lates average heart rate. You also need to determine training zones based
on your LTHR. To find this number, do a 10-mile time trial, riding as
hard and steady as possible. Your average heart rate for this effort is your
LTHR. Then use the table to determine your personal training zones.
For best results, do the time trial when you're rested and motivated, and
give it your all. Use a flat course on a day with calm weather.

Find Your Training Zones

ZONE	% OF LTHR	PACE
1	65–81	Recovery
2	82–88	Endurance
3	89–93	Tempo
4	94–99	Threshold
5	100–102	Threshold+

For example, if you time trial at a heart rate of 160 beats per minute,
your training ranges would be: Zone 1, 104 to 130; Zone 2, 131 to 141;
Zone 3, 142 to 149; Zone 4, 150 to 159; Zone 5, 160 to 163.

26 Weeks to Peak Condition

It's Friel's contention that even if you have very little time to train, you can still go from zero to top-gun condition in the first half of the season, then have great performances in important events. His system requires minimal training knowledge or experience and no big dietary changes.

Friel uses periodization. His plan is based on 4-week blocks of time during which you work on different aspects of fitness. The repetitive pattern is 3 weeks of training followed by a week of rest and recovery. "Don't get impatient during the R-and-R weeks," he warns. "They're vital for measuring progress and avoiding setbacks due to injury, illness, or overtraining."

Note that the total suggested riding time doesn't add up to the total recommended training time. Fill the remaining time with easy to moderate rides for recovery or endurance. Also, weight training greatly benefits performance. But remember—the goal is to ride stronger, not develop bulky muscles. That's why the weight workouts are brief and focused. Good exercises for cycling include leg presses, stepups, seated rows, dumbbell rows, bench presses, lat pulldowns, pushups, pullups, and abdominal crunches. Choose a weight that allows you to do the suggested number of reps.

Get Started

WEEK 1

Train: 3 to 4 hours total; emphasize fast cadence (90 to 100 rpm)

Ride: 1 hour on a rolling course, with at least 50 percent of the time spent in Zone 2 (avoid Zones 4 and 5); or 45 minutes indoors, using gears to simulate hills; repeat if you have time

Cross-train: Easy for 20 minutes (run, swim, cross-country ski, or stairclimb); repeat

Weights: Complete four sets of 20 to 30 reps in two workouts

WEEK 2

Train: 3 hours and 30 minutes to 4 hours and 30 minutes total; emphasize fast cadence

Ride: Same as Week 1

Cross-train: Same as Week 1

Weights: Complete six sets of 20 to 30 reps in two workouts

WEEK 3

Train: 4 to 5 hours total; emphasize fast cadence

Ride: Same as Week 1

Cross-train: Same as Week 1

Weights: Complete six to eight sets of 20 to 30 reps in two workouts

WEEK 4

Rest: Decrease total time of Week 3 by 25 percent and rest; establish an aerobic baseline with test

Ride: Total of 2 to 3 hours in Zone 2

Cross-train: Same as Week 1

Weights: Complete four sets of 20 to 30 reps in two workouts

Test: 45 minutes total; warm up 10 minutes on indoor trainer, then ride 3 miles at 9 to 11 beats below LTHR; record gear/resistance and time; spin easily to cool down

Build Strength

WEEK 5

Train: 4 hours total; complete a long ride of 1 hour and 15 minutes to 1 hour and 45 minutes

Ride: 45 minutes on a rolling course, with 50 percent in Zone 2; avoid Zones 4 and 5; stay seated on hills. Or 30 minutes indoors, using gears to simulate hills; repeat if time

Long ride: 1 hour and 15 minutes on a rolling course or do 55 minutes indoors, using gears to simulate hills

Weights: Complete six sets of four to eight reps in two workouts

Indoor trainer: 30 minutes total; do three 30-second steady accelerations to 120 rpm with 1-minute recoveries. Then do three 30-second sessions (each leg) of one-leg pedaling with 1-minute recoveries; repeat one or two times, or cross-train if bored

WEEK 6

Train: 4 hours and 45 minutes total; complete a long ride of 1 hour and 30 minutes to 2 hours

Ride: 45 minutes on a rolling course, with 50 percent in Zone 2; avoid Zones 4 and 5; stay seated on hills. Or 30 minutes indoors, using gears to simulate hills; repeat if time

Long ride: 1 hour and 30 minutes on a rolling course or do 1 hour and 5 minutes indoors, using gears to simulate hills

Weights: Complete six to eight sets of four to eight reps in two workouts

Indoor trainer: Same as Week 5, but for a total of 45 minutes

WEEK 7

Train: 5 hours and 30 minutes total; complete a long ride of 1 hour and 45 minutes to 2 hours and 15 minutes

Ride: 45 minutes on a rolling course with 50 percent in Zone 2; avoid Zones 4 and 5; stay seated on hills. Or 30 minutes indoors, using gears to simulate hills; repeat if time

Long ride: 1 hour and 45 minutes on a rolling course or do 1 hour and 15 minutes indoors, using gears to simulate hills

Weights: Same as Week 6

Indoor trainer: Same as Week 6

WEEK 8

Rest: Decrease total time of Week 7 by 25 percent and rest; test aerobic fitness

Rides: Total of 3 to 4 hours in Zone 2

Weights: Complete four sets of four to eight reps in two workouts

Indoor trainer: Same as Week 6

Test: Same as Week 4

Boost Endurance

WEEK 9

Train: 4 hours and 30 minutes total; complete a long ride of 1 hour and 30 minutes to 2 hours

Ride: 45 minutes, as stated in Week 1; repeat if time

Long ride: 1 hour and 30 minutes on a rolling course, with 50 percent in Zone 2; avoid Zones 4 and 5; stay seated on hills. Or ride 1 hour and 5 minutes indoors, using gears to simulate hills

Weights: Complete six sets of 8 to 15 reps in two workouts

Skills: 45 minutes total; for off-road, work on hopping, slalom, jumping, etc.; for road, work on high-speed cornering skills; if indoors, practice one-leg pedaling and steady accelerations

WEEK 10

Train: 5 hours and 15 minutes total; complete a long ride of 2 hours to 2 hours and 30 minutes

Ride: Same as Week 9

Weights: Same as Week 9

Skills: Same as Week 9

WEEK 11

Train: 5 hours and 30 minutes total; complete a long ride of 2 hours to 2 hours and 30 minutes

Ride: Same as Week 9

Weights: Same as Week 9

Skills: Same as Week 9, but for 1 hour

WEEK 12

Rest: Decrease total time of Week 11 by 25 percent and rest; test aerobic fitness

Ride: 1 hour on a rolling course, with 50 percent in Zone 2; avoid Zones 4 and 5. Or ride 45 minutes indoors, using gears to simulate hills; repeat if time

Weights: Complete four sets of 8 to 15 reps for the week in two workouts

Test: Same as Week 4

Skills: Same as Week 9

Climb

WEEK 13

Train: 5 hours total; complete a long ride of 2 hours to 2 hours and 30 minutes

Long ride: 2 hours on moderately hilly course in Zones 1 through 4 (avoid Zone 5). Or ride 1 hour and 30 minutes indoors, using gears to simulate hills

Hills: Ride 45 minutes on course with long climbs, with 10 to 20 percent of time in Zones 4 and 5. Or simulate indoors for 35 minutes

Tempo: Warm up for 10 minutes, then ride 20 minutes in Zone 3; relax and pedal smoothly

Weights: Complete two sets of 40 to 60 reps in one workout

WEEK 14

Train: 5 hours and 30 minutes total; complete a long ride of 2 hours to 2 hours and 30 minutes

Ride: Same as Week 13

Weights: Same as Week 13

WEEK 15

Train: 6 hours; complete a long ride of 2 hours and 30 minutes
to 3 hours

Ride: Same as Week 13, but add 30 minutes to long ride

Weights: Same as Week 13

WEEK 16

Rest: Decrease total time of Week 15 by 25 percent and rest; test aerobic
fitness

Ride: 1 hour on rolling course, with 50 percent of time in Zone 2 (avoid
Zones 3 through 5). Or ride 45 minutes indoors; repeat if time

Weights: For Weeks 16 through 26, do two sets of each exercise only
once per week (set one, 12 to 15 reps; set two, 6 to 8 reps)

Test: Same as Week 4

Get Specific

WEEK 17

Train: 5 hours and 30 minutes total; complete a long ride of 2 hours and
30 minutes on a hilly course (can be with a group)

Long ride: 2 hours and 30 minutes in the hills, 10 to 20 percent of time
in Zones 4 and 5. Or ride 1 hour and 50 minutes indoors and use
gears to simulate hills. If training for a century, add 30 minutes and
ride in Zones 2 and 3 on a rolling course

Cruise intervals: 1 hour total; on road or trainer, warm up 10 to 15
minutes, then do three to four 6-minute repeats in Zones 4 and 5
(2-minute recoveries). Relax, listen to breathing, and pedal
smoothly

Recovery: Ride for 45 minutes in Zone 1; repeat if time

WEEK 18

Train: 5 hours and 30 minutes total; complete a long ride of 2 hours and
30 minutes on a hilly course (can be with a group)

Ride: Same as Week 17

WEEK 19

Train: 5 hours and 30 minutes total; complete a long ride of 2 hours and
30 minutes on a hilly course (can be with a group)

Ride: Same as Week 17

WEEK 20

Rest: Ride four times, but otherwise rest; test aerobic fitness

Recovery: Ride 1 hour in Zone 1; repeat if time

Test: Warm up 10 to 15 minutes, then ride a 10-mile time trial on the road; note average heart rate and recompute training zones

Ride Fast

WEEK 21

Train: 6 hours total; complete a long ride of at least 2 hours and 30 minutes in the hills (can be with a group)

Long ride: 2 hours and 30 minutes with a group in varying terrain, according to how you feel. If training for a century, add 1 hour and ride in Zones 2 and 3 on a rolling course

Threshold: Warm up 10 to 15 minutes. Then ride continuously for 20 minutes in Zones 4 and 5. Relax, listen to breathing, pedal smoothly. 1 hour total

Recovery: Ride 45 minutes in Zone 1 on road or indoors; repeat if time

WEEK 22

Train: 6 hours total; complete a long ride of at least 2 hours and 30 minutes in the hills (can be with a group)

Ride: Same as Week 21

WEEK 23

Train: 6 hours total; complete a long ride of at least 2 hours and 30 minutes in the hills (can be with a group)

Ride: Same as Week 21, but add 5 to 10 minutes to threshold ride

WEEK 24

Rest: Ride four times, but otherwise rest; test aerobic fitness

Recovery: Ride 1 hour in Zone 1 on road or indoors; repeat if time

Test: Same as Week 20

Peak

WEEK 25

Train: 6 hours total; complete a long ride of at least 2 hours and 30 minutes (can be a race) and do a 1-hour-and-30-minute fast group ride

Long ride: 2 hours and 30 minutes with a group in varying terrain, according to how you feel. If training for a century, add 1 hour and ride in Zones 2 and 3 on a rolling course

Recovery: Ride for 45 minutes in Zone 1 on road or indoors. Repeat if time

Fast group: Ride 1 hour and 30 minutes in varying terrain, including several minutes in Zone 5

WEEK 26

Train: 6 hours total; complete a long ride of at least 2 hours and 30 minutes (can be a race) and do a 1-hour-and-30-minute fast group ride

Ride: Same as Week 25

14
Mixed Training

In the days of wool shorts and nail-on cleats, cyclists planned yearly training according to tradition and whim. Rest in the winter, pile on base miles in early spring, then begin intervals to pump up for summer racing.

Riders adjusted their training based on how they felt or how fast the group was going that day. This produced unpredictable peaks. Sometimes you were flying and sometimes you had to struggle—but you were never quite sure which to expect.

Periodization training was developed to remedy the unpredictability. The idea is to work on certain energy systems—endurance, lactate threshold, power—at specific times of the year. Each has its place in carefully charted training rhythms that ebb and flow with the months. Joe Friel's program in chapter 13 is a good basic example of how to train in periods.

Periodization works. The only drawback is that some plans are so regimented that while one energy system is being trained, the others atrophy. For example, riders putting in major miles at an aerobic pace may find they can't go fast. Conversely, building max VO_2 (maximal oxygen consumption) with gut-wrenching intervals saps endurance—and energy. Who cares how high you've pushed your lactate threshold if you're too tired to ride?

Beneficial Blend

Now there's a school of thought that promises periodization's strengths while sidestepping its risks. Simply stated, "mixed training" blends all the energy systems all year-round.

"You blend different energy systems during a period when you're emphasizing a specific one," former national coaching director Chris Carmichael explains. "We're getting away from the extreme specialization of the past." Finding the optimum mix isn't simple, though. It's certainly easier being a one-trick pony. "That's why coaching is an art," says Carmichael.

If you're ready to become an artist, here are some guidelines.

Time trial regularly. The ability to roll a big gear steadily for 20 minutes at 90 to 95 percent of maximum heart rate is basic to performance cycling as well as fitness. Whether you're chasing another rider, climbing a long hill, or racing a thunderstorm home, your body needs to be an energy pump capable of long efforts that hover precariously at the upper limits.

"The national team rides time trials during every phase of training," Carmichael says. "The riders do 15 kilometers (nearly 10 miles) all-out about every 5 weeks. The thinking is that athletes of that caliber should be able to time trial at top speed any time of the year."

Recreational riders may want to time trial once every 3 to 4 weeks. If a local club has a monthly 10-mile time trial, that's perfect.

Work on speed. Sprinting isn't just for sprinters. "Do some sprints every week of the year," Carmichael suggests. They'll recruit your fast-twitch muscle fibers and improve your pedal stroke. In addition, regular speedwork will raise your average rpm and, thus, your speed. For instance, suppose you increase your cadence by 5 rpm—say, from 90 to 95. In a 100-inch gear, this translates to a speed increase of nearly 1.5 mph. That's roughly equivalent to adding aero bars or disk wheels.

Speedwork doesn't necessarily mean crunching big gears. Start with fast spinning in the small chainring when you have a tailwind or are on a gradual downhill. Or spin out a low gear for 15 seconds every 5 or 10 minutes on endurance rides. Then graduate to sprinting for road signs while on training rides with friends. Keep it fun.

Do a competitive ride at least every 2 weeks. It doesn't have to be a race, although racing uses every energy system (endurance to go the distance, power on hills, time-trialing ability to close gaps or get away from the pack, and speed in the sprint or when jumping out of corners). If you race frequently, your training mix takes care of itself.

But any competitive ride works. For instance, when out on your mountain bike with the guys, you jam up short hills, time trial on longer climbs, and keep a brisk pace for a couple of hours. It's all made palatable by the sauce of friendly competition.

Forget hard-day/easy-day training. The pattern, Carmichael argues, should be 3 hard days followed by several easier ones. This will teach your body to sustain high output, conditioning you for multi-day rides or even stage races. But the hard days should be hard in a variety of ways. For instance, Day 1 could be a short ride with sprints, Day 2 an endurance ride, Day 3 devoted to intervals. Follow with several days of easy spinning to recover.

The Freedom Factor

Besides making you a better rider, mixed training has two additional benefits. First, it adds variety to each week's workouts, freeing you from a boring rut. You can still set aside several weeks to emphasize a certain energy system—speed, for instance, or power—but variety will help both your head and legs. Second, you can escape the traditional steady diet of early-season endurance rides when days are still short and the weather is usually bad. When you are free to build a base over the whole season in concert with other skills, you won't have to grind out too many 4-hour rides in February sleet.

But hold on a second before you abandon periodization. Mixed training isn't the only answer—it's just one method of distributing intensity and distance over weeks and months. You still need to follow basic rules of training such as getting sufficient rest and recovery. If there were only one program that worked for all riders, every race would end in a photo finish. All approaches have the defects of their virtues.

The solution? Mix your training but also focus on specific skills at appropriate times of the year. For instance, sprint every week, but in the early season when the emphasis is on endurance, make sprints part of longer rides. In June, when you need top speed for summer events, devote 1 day each week solely to sprints, alternating all-out efforts and long recoveries. Mix it up.

PART FOUR

Special Workouts

15
Speed

Many cyclists never practice sprinting because they see no need for speed. It's certainly a lot easier to cruise at a steady, comfortable pace. After all, speed is for racers and simply isn't necessary for people who ride for fitness and recreation.

Think again. Speed is a main constituent of cycling ability, and it does have many uses. For example, group rides often feature spirited jumps and sprints to city-limit signs. In town, you may need a burst of speed to hold your place in traffic or get safely through a yellow light. Even on a long ride where endurance reigns supreme, speed training pays off. When that country dog comes boiling out of its yard, bent on mayhem, a quick acceleration is usually the best defense. If you can keep the mutt behind you until you pass the invisible boundary of its territory, you'll be safe.

In these and similar situations, the skill is the same. You must accelerate to high speed, then hold that speed for a few seconds. Obviously, this is essential in racing. But beyond the practical benefits, you'll find that riding fast is just plain fun. Good bicycles and fit bodies beg to fly; don't condemn yours to a pedestrian pace. Fortunately, anyone can become significantly faster, and developing this talent is easier than you may expect.

Speedwork

Conventional interval training helps you ride faster, but its main objectives are the development of aerobic and anaerobic capacity. When you do intervals, each intense effort is followed by easier riding that allows only partial recovery, then you go hard again. Speedwork is different. The hard efforts are very hard, virtually as hard as you can go, but they are brief and separated by enough time for complete recovery. For instance, just 15 to 30 seconds of intense riding may be followed by as much as 5 minutes of easy spinning. The emphasis is on acceleration and leg speed, not heart rate. You always start from Zone 1, but the ending heart rate isn't important and, in fact, will vary depending on the length of the sprint.

Steve Bauer, Canada's all-time best road rider, won many races with

Good sprinting form includes a centered upper body.

his blazing speed in the final 200 meters. He suggests doing speedwork once or twice a week year-round. Simply incorporate it into a routine ride. Warm up for at least 15 minutes, then do five to eight sprints of up to 30 seconds each with full recovery between them. Use gears that you won't completely spin out, and be sure to concentrate on the elements of good technique described below. Afterward, finish the ride at an easy pace to cool down.

This whole workout takes only about an hour. After several weeks, there should be a noticeable improvement in your top-end speed and your ability to hold it longer. You'll find it easier to make that light or escape that menacing dog.

Spin City

Authorities say that speed can be developed in two ways: by increasing cadence (pedaling faster) or by increasing power (pedaling harder) so that you can use a bigger gear. So far, so good—but there's a third key to quickness that is often neglected: technique. Without efficient form, a cyclist with the speed of a cheetah and the power of a Mack truck will waste most of it on flailing legs, flying elbows, and bobbing shoulders. Speed depends on cadence and technique, so let's see how to improve them.

The most basic way to cultivate fast, smooth leg speed is to spin low-to-moderate gears at high rpm. You need to work on this before starting formal speedwork. If your normal cruising cadence is around 90 rpm, start there and gradually increase it to 100, 110, 120—until your legs lose coordination and you're bouncing on the saddle. Ease back about 5 rpm and hold it there for a few seconds, then inch it up again. Repeat this sequence several times. After just a few sessions, your maximum cadence and the fastest smooth cadence you can sustain will both be greater.

Use gradual downhills to help get your cadence up. Instead of shifting into bigger gears as you descend, stay in lower gears and let gravity help turn your legs into a blur. A similar trick is to use lower gears when you catch a tailwind, then pedal for several minutes at high rpm.

Then move on to low-gear intervals. Instead of using customary gears such as 53×16T at 90 rpm to develop power, use 39×16T at 120 rpm. One-minute intervals done this way will continue to improve coordination as they condition your cardiovascular system and fast-twitch muscle fibers, two key ingredients of a good sprint.

When you start using these techniques, your pedal stroke is bound to feel choppy and somewhat uncoordinated. Overcome this by focusing on relaxation. Mentally separate your upper and lower body. Keep your shoulders and arms loose and quiet. Try to confine all motion to your legs, which will help keep your hips from bouncing. Encourage smoothness by thinking "pedal faster" not "pedal harder" as rpm tops out. This approach works anytime you want to turn the crankset quicker, no matter what gear you're in.

Technique Tips

Bauer has identified three major technique flaws that show up in most cyclists when they're sprinting out of the saddle. By avoiding these, your ability to accelerate and then hold your speed will be much improved.

First, riders tend to move their upper bodies too much. Bauer explains that your back is like a fulcrum and shouldn't move. When your upper body is kept almost perfectly still, it serves as a brace for the power of your legs. Your arms should move only enough to let the bike sway from side to side in rhythm with your pedal strokes.

Second, cyclists tend to move their weight too far forward. When you stand to sprint, your shoulders should be only as far forward as the front axle, Bauer says. Lean forward more, and you'll encounter several speed-sapping problems. You'll have too much weight on your front wheel, which will make the bike unstable and hard to handle. Your hips will be too far forward in relation to the crankset, which means you won't be able to get as much leverage on the pedals. And your head will be down, making it difficult to see where you're going—not smart when you're pushing for maximum speed.

Finally, cyclists tend to use their upper body incorrectly. When sprinting, you should pull on the handlebar with a rowing motion to balance the power of your legs. If you don't, the bike will flop around dangerously, and some power will go into wasted motion instead of pedaling.

16
Power

In cycling, power and speed are related but they also have distinct definitions. Speed is the ability to sprint to high rpm in whatever gear you're using, then hold that red-line velocity for a short time. Power, on the other hand, is more related to strength than to quickness. It's what gets you over steep climbs without resorting to your granny gear and what helps you hold an impressive pace into a tough headwind. It's the ability to keep the crankarms turning when the resistance rises. A great example of where power and speed merge is when you're sprinting in a big gear.

Power has a precise meaning to physiologists. It's defined as force multiplied by velocity, and physics says that the power required to overcome air drag is proportional to the cube of the velocity.

So what does this mean when you're on your bike? Simply that if you want to increase your speed from 20 to 25 mph, you need to *double* your power output. And if you want to double your speed from 15 to 30 mph, your power must increase *eightfold*. Now think about English pro Chris Boardman, who set a world record by riding more than 34 miles in 1 hour around an indoor velodrome. That's power.

Power lets you ride more explosively, too. You can sprint in a bigger gear, which lets you cover ground faster. You know you need to work on power when you encounter these problems: You can't sprint in a gear that's big enough to make you competitive; you can't maintain the group's speed when you reach the front of a paceline; you have trouble getting back into the paceline following your pull; you struggle to get going again if something slows you on a hill; you find it impossible to accelerate during a climb; headwinds force you into low gears; and rides that make you frequently change pace leave you overly tired.

Power Training

Working on power means sometimes riding with a relatively low cadence. Instead of the leg-blurring spin of speedwork sprints, where cadences may exceed 120 rpm, you may find yourself down around 70 rpm or even lower. This is especially true on hills, where you intentionally remain in a gear that makes you drive the pedals, rather than shift lower and spin as you would during a typical ride.

There is a wide variety of ways to develop power. One is with hard accelerations in a big gear. For instance, roll along at 40 rpm in 53×16T, stay seated, and accelerate as hard as you can for 10 seconds. Recover fully by spinning a much lower gear. Repeat five to eight times. You can accomplish much the same thing by riding in rolling terrain and charging up short hills in the saddle without shifting down or letting your cadence drop (or you can even try to increase it). On longer climbs, shift to a higher gear halfway up, stand, and pound over the top. Or repeatedly slow and accelerate all the way up. Alternate sitting and standing, and always finish with a sprint. When facing a long headwind stretch, select a moderately big gear and keep your cadence at a steady 80 rpm as you bore through the invisible wall.

Sound like fun? Well, it's not easy to develop the cardiovascular fitness, muscle strength, and energy systems that power requires. Much of this work is in heart-rate Zone 4, around the lactate threshold. You may find that initial workouts leave you feeling hammered. Stick with it. Just one such training session per week will increase your power quite quickly, especially if you haven't been riding with this type of exertion.

For best gains and to avoid overtraining, be sure to plan easy recovery rides for the days before and after a power workout. A training schedule that many riders follow calls for Monday rest after lots of weekend riding, speedwork on Tuesday, steady endurance riding on Wednesday, power work on Thursday, and an easy spin for recovery on Friday.

In addition, cyclists whose events put a premium on power (including time trialists, criterium specialists, trackies, and people who race in hilly terrain) almost always emphasize weight training in their winter programs. Heavy lifting, especially squats and leg presses, builds a power base that can then be increased through the specific on-bike training that was just described.

17
Endurance

Long rides are an excellent adventure for all cyclists. Maybe you can't time trial at 30 mph, ride a stage race, or win at mountain biking, but you can set a personal distance record. To show you how to make your cyclecomputer flash its biggest number ever, just listen to endurance guru John Hughes, a Race Across America finisher, a cycling coach, and the managing director of the UltraMarathon Cycling Association. Whatever distance represents your personal goal, Hughes knows how to help you get there.

Making the Commitment

"Begin by committing to a specific goal," says Hughes. "You can't be half-hearted and say, 'Oh, maybe I'll try a century sometime this year.' Then once you decide on an event, do it—no second thoughts."

Of course, the commitment doesn't end with a promise—that's just the beginning. You need to pony up at least three training rides a week, the minimum to gain fitness and accomplish a long ride. "Plan two endurance rides weekly of at least 2 hours," says Hughes. The third ride can be shorter and more intense—the type of training that will raise your cruising speed.

The biggest challenge for most endurance-oriented riders is finding enough time to train. Search your schedule for available slots. Ride while the kids are at gymnastics, or use your bike to get to your in-laws for dinner. A great solution for many riders is to use their bikes for daily transportation.

"Try commuting to work by bike 1 or 2 days a week," says Hughes. "Maybe you can make a deal with your boss. If you work longer on Tuesday, you can leave early another day. Try to fit riding into daylight hours, not after dark. Too many bad things can happen then—you're better off on an indoor trainer. The exception is early-morning darkness. Traffic is much lighter at 5:00 A.M., so it's safer."

Commuting has been the key to consistent training for numerous long-distance riders. Perhaps the most famous example is Pete Penseyres, the two-time winner of the Race Across America. For several years, the foundation of his endurance was his daily ride to work and back, which totaled 60 hilly miles. Your commute doesn't have to be this long to be effective, but if it seems too short, simply scout out a less direct course that adds some distance.

Once you've commited to a training schedule, use these tips to follow through.

Gradually build your mileage. The rule of thumb, no matter what level you're starting at or what distance you want to reach, is to increase mileage by 10 percent each week. Once you can comfortably finish a ride that equals 75 percent of your target distance, you're ready. For example, if you're shooting for a century, build to a training ride of 75 miles. If you do it right, "you'll finish tired but excited about life and riding your bike," Hughes says.

If your goal is a long off-road event, don't use distance as your training yardstick. Instead, aim for 75 percent of the total projected time.

Mimic the event. "It's easier to get out there with friends," says Hughes. "Training should mimic the event, however. If you plan to draft in a century, practice pack riding. If you've challenged yourself to ride solo on the road or you're planning a long off-road ride, get used to hammering by yourself in the wind.

"The same thinking holds true if you've picked a hilly event—train on climbs. You'll do better on the big day if your preparation has mirrored it. Also, practice changing flats, getting food out of your jersey pockets, and eating while riding. You don't want any surprises."

Choose equipment early. "Go for gear that increases comfort rather than speed," says Hughes. "For instance, set up your aero handlebar to give you a higher, more relaxed position. Raise the stem and put risers under the arm rests. Get everything dialed in halfway through training and don't change anything after that. Also, tailor your equipment choices to the event. For instance, install fenders if you expect rain."

Carrying everything you need on a long ride can be a challenge. Use a large, expandable seatbag to carry two spare tire tubes, a patch kit, tire levers, a multitool, and arm/leg warmers (if needed). Roll a rain jacket tightly and strap it underneath the bag. Then stuff your jersey's rear pockets. Balance heavy items such as energy bars by putting them in the left and right pockets. Use the pocket in the center for light items such as lip balm, sunscreen, ID, money, and your route map. Use a plastic bag to protect these items from sweat and rain.

Pace yourself. Before you begin the ride, think about your pace. "Imagine how you'll feel at the halfway point," says Hughes. "If you ride the first half of the distance as if you were already that tired, you'll have enough left to finish strong. Joining a paceline can make an event more fun, but don't get in over your head. It's easy to get suckered into riding too fast too early. Maintain your best pace."

On the other hand, don't waste time. "Stops at stores or rest stops in events aren't for rest," says Hughes. "Don't sit down and eat. Instead, fill your bottles and stuff some food in your jersey pockets so that you can munch as you're rolling down the road. Spend 5 minutes, max, for any stop."

Tank up. Food and fluids are crucial for long-distance rides. Hughes's rules of thumb are simple: "If you aren't urinating at least once every 2 to 3 hours, you aren't drinking enough. And you need to consume 300 calories every hour of the ride. Slug down energy drinks and eat energy bars, bananas, or cookies. If you don't eat enough, it'll get ugly."

For an unsupported ride in remote areas, use a backpack-style hydration system to reduce the risk of running out of fluids. For mountain biking in the backcountry, consider packing a water filter.

Divide to conquer. A long ride is as much a mental challenge as a physical feat. Hughes plans for success this way: "Divide the ride into thirds. The first third, you'll feel great, the middle third will drag, but in the final third, you'll be like a horse heading for the barn. If you realize that the middle part is mentally the hardest, you can overcome those feelings. Also, ride in the present. Don't worry about the strain of the last climb or how hard it will become when the route turns into the wind in 5 miles. Concentrate on the scenery or the act of riding the bike. Set short-term goals instead of the total distance that remains. Think about making it to the next town or rest stop, then the town or rest stop after that."

Hughes saves his favorite tip for last. "In the final few miles of the ride, I spend all my time planning what I'll have for dinner," he says. "It's a great reward for accomplishing the goal."

18
Block Training

Dean Golich, a cycling coach in Colorado Springs, has a different slant on training. His formula is simple: Throw away your heart-rate monitor. Forget about alternating hard and easy days. Just go as hard as you can, and do it for 2 or 3 days in a row before you rest. He calls this block training. It's perfect for riders who want to train but have limited time.

It sounds like a recipe for exhaustion and overtraining, but some followers have had great success. Golich's clients include U.S. time-trial record holder Mari Holden and U.S. hour record holder Norm Alvis. While this program defies conventional training wisdom, it works for these national-class riders and it could be right for you, too, if you're trying to pack significant improvement into limited training time. Consider it along with all of the other advice in this book as you design your own program.

Gruesome Twosome
Golich's approach is based on two heretical recommendations. First, shelve your heart-rate monitor. "You don't need it for hard training," Golich argues, "because there's little correlation between heart rate and power output. If cyclists look at their heart rates during hard efforts and see low numbers compared to their perceived exertion, they're supposed to stop the interval session and ride home. But when I examine SRM PowerMeter data, which measures output in watts, often they're putting

out more power than a day or two earlier when their heart rates were higher. Heart rate isn't a reliable indicator of power."

What about the intricate training zones so beloved of heart-rate training gurus? They aren't necessary, Golich says. In fact, Golich recognizes only three levels of training effort: easy, medium, and hard, determined subjectively.

Heresy number two: Train hard several days in a row. This block training is key to Golich's program. Instead of alternating strenuous and easy days, his riders train ferociously hard for 2 or 3 consecutive days, then rest for 2 or 3 more days by spinning at an easy pace. When they feel recovered, they put in another 2 or 3 intense days. Golich promises that this schedule won't lead to overtraining. "Pro racers go all out for 3 weeks in a row in the Tour de France," he notes, "and if they rest properly after the Tour, they're flying."

Tough Intervals

Golich usually prescribes just one level of effort for intervals: as hard as you can. He doesn't want you to start a bit easier so you can last the distance without undue suffering. "Don't pace yourself," he says. "If you're doing 5-minute efforts, start the interval flat out. You'll be struggling at the end, but that's okay. That's when you get the adaptation."

To illustrate, Golich invokes what he calls the 30-mph rule: If you never go 30 mph, you'll never go 30 mph. Don't expect to do well at any particular speed—be it 30, 25, 20, or even 15 mph—if you consistently train at slower speeds. If your goal is 30 mph, start your interval at 30. As you get tired, your speed will decrease but your effort will not.

"If you do intervals this way, next week or next month you'll be able to hold the speed longer," Golich says. You'll feel fatigue, but it's temporary. It isn't overtraining (the rest days ensure that), so tough it out.

Easy Days

Golich has scientific backing for his program. In a study done at the University of Wyoming in Laramie, eight top cyclists were subjected to 3 weeks of hard training. Each week included eight maximum-effort interval sessions, a sprint workout, and a 5-minute all-out test. Cycling performance improved significantly during training and increased even more after 2 weeks of recovery.

That covers the hard, lung-blowing aspect of Golich's program, but what about easy and medium efforts? An easy pace is for recovery days.

When you go easy, Golich wants you to go really easy—no pressure on the pedals. These days are great opportunities to ride at the pace of people who aren't as strong as you—maybe a spouse, child, or friend who is new to cycling.

Golich occasionally prescribes intervals at medium pace, which he defines as the effort you can maintain for an hour. They're great for increasing time-trialing ability or cruising speed. A typical workout consists of three repeats of 15 minutes each separated by 5 minutes of easy spinning.

Warning Signs

Any program this tough has dangers. Before attempting it, be sure you have a good aerobic base of at least 8 weeks of progressively longer rides. Save your knees during the hard intervals by using gears that let you keep your cadence in the 80- to 100-rpm range, even at the end of the effort. Shift to an easier gear, if necessary, to prevent your cadence from bogging down. You want to keep both effort and rpm high.

Finally, monitor your enthusiasm for this program. If you experience symptoms of overtraining (such as poor performance, insomnia, loss of appetite, or an I-don't-care attitude), return to steady, moderately paced rides until you recover.

Far from being effective only for elite riders, Golich's program may work if you have minimal time to train. It gives you all the intensity training you need in a short time. You can train hard on the weekend plus either Friday or Monday, then spend the rest of the week recovering as you turn your attention to work and other matters.

19
Powerful Mountain Biking

For years, road riders have been poked, prodded, and bled in the name of science. But only recently have the folks in the white coats started to make mountain bikers squirm around in the petri dish of athletic performance. The results of one important study are complete—and they may change the way you train.

The study was conducted at the Olympic Training Center in Colorado Springs by researchers Ed Burke, Ph.D., cycling physiologist and director of the exercise-science program at the University of Colorado, also in Colorado Springs; Sharon McDowell, Ph.D., and Rebecca Milot-Bradford. "One goal of the study," reports Dr. McDowell, "was to see whether cycling abilities measured in the lab carry over to performance in the real world of racing." To find out, the subjects—14 male expert-level mountain bikers—performed a series of grueling lab tests carefully designed to measure four important cycling attributes: power at lactate threshold, anaerobic power, technique, and upper-body strength.

To determine the intensity level that can be sustained in a steady effort (power at lactate threshold), the riders labored through an ergometer (stationary bicycle) test that revealed how much power they could produce for long periods of time. To check how quickly power tailed off because of fatigue (for instance, how you might feel when riding hard over a series of short hills), riders hammered five consecutive all-out 30-second efforts with minimal rest between each sprint (anaerobic power). In order to. determine the impact of technique, the researchers measured bike-handling skills by timing the riders in a section of an actual race, followed by a time trial over difficult terrain. This determined the impact of technique. To measure upper-body strength, the riders did as many bench rows as possible using 35 percent of their body weight.

Power and Performance

The measurement of steady power output (power at lactate threshold) was the best yardstick of race performance, according to Dr. McDowell. "That was significantly related to performance for all three races used for comparison," she reports. "The anaerobic data, the repeated 30-second sprints, were less clearly related but were significant for one race that included lots of hard climbing and gnarly descending."

Technique also correlated to all three race performances. Upper-body strength only showed a correlation in the final race. Dr. McDowell speculates that this may be an indication that over the course of a long season, overall body strength becomes more important.

Unlike many studies, this one went far beyond the usual lab data. For instance, McDowell analyzed each subject's training diary to see how the intensity and volume of workouts correlated with race results. In general, "the better riders had a lot more structure in their training than the slower ones. What this means is if you're new to the sport, it helps to get a coach to show you how to set up your season plan and get the most from your time on the bike."

If you don't have a coach and want to improve the four physical attributes measured in the study, here are workouts that Dr. McDowell suggests.

Turn up the wattage. Off-road races are a bit like road time trials, where pack tactics don't count. You just go as hard as you can for the distance. Assuming you have a good fitness base, the following three workouts will increase the wattage you can produce during efforts of 30 minutes to an hour. They can be done on a mountain bike on smooth terrain (such as fire roads) or on a road bike. Warm up for at least 20 minutes before starting.

1. Ride hard for 15 minutes at an intensity you can barely maintain for the distance. Spin easily for 10 minutes to recover. Increase by one repeat each week until you reach three.

2. Find a long, moderate hill that takes about 30 minutes to climb. Climb it twice a week at a steady, hard pace. If there are no long hills nearby, ride hard for 30 minutes on a flat road, into the wind.

3. Ride a local time trial once a week. There's no substitute for competition to make you work hard. Don't have a road bike? Ride your mountain bike. Sure, you'll go slower than riders on fancy time-trial bikes, but what's important is your own improvement.

Increase your pain threshold. Once you've built steady-state power, work on your ability to survive repeated hard bursts, such as when you're riding over a series of small hills. The goal is to raise your anaerobic tolerance. After a warmup, do three 30-second intervals with a minute rest between each one. Pedal easily for 10 minutes, then do another set of three intervals. As your recovery improves, increase each effort to 1 minute. Do these intervals on flat sections as well as hills.

Get technical. In the study, riders were timed over a section of race course that took about 10 minutes. The gap between an average competitor and an elite/pro rider was about 90 seconds. This doesn't sound like much, but over a 2-hour race, Joe Average could expect to lose a whopping 18 minutes to the top riders on technical acumen alone.

The message is clear. "You need to spend significant time on tech-

Ned Overend combines power and technique to get the most from off-road training.

nical trails," says Dr. McDowell. "Ride and re-ride tough sections. Get coaching to help you improve your skills. Consider videotaping these practice sessions for later analysis. Train with better riders and follow their lines." And for a ton of bike-handling secrets and technique tips, check out world-champion mountain bike racer Ned Overend's book *Mountain Bike like a Champion* (Rodale Press, 1999).

Pump iron. You've heard it before and it can't be emphasized enough—upper-body strength is important for mountain biking. Incorporate weight training into your winter program. Then maintain strength by doing crunches, pushups and pullups twice a week no matter where you are during the season.

PART FIVE

Off-Season
Training

20
Weight Training

Until the 1980s, cyclists rarely lifted weights. In fact, weight training was spurned by most endurance athletes, and the physique of choice was the marathoning ideal—lean to the point of emaciation. Few cyclists had weight-training experience, and most coaches didn't believe it could help riders improve. Iron was anathema.

But now, in one of training theory's periodic about-faces, everyone is pumping iron enthusiastically. What happened? On the recreational side, cyclists got tired of wimpy-looking upper bodies. Buffness became cool. (It's probably no coincidence that the move to weight training coincided with the popularity of form-fitting spandex.) Vanity aside, the Eastern European cyclists of the 1980s demonstrated that with strength comes speed. The great East German and Soviet sprinters were built like Greek gods.

For long-distance riders, weight training became a way to condition the upper body for the rigors of hours in the saddle. It was thought that the best way to do this was simply to ride, and the arms, shoulders, neck, and back would adapt. Cyclists now realize that weights can effectively build the required strength, making the season's first long rides more comfortable and allowing endurance to improve at a faster rate.

Despite this new enthusiasm for weight training, however, findings from the National Strength and Conditioning Association indicate that some cyclists are going about it in ways that may be less effective than they could be. Circuit training, high repetitions, endless squats—all have their outspoken advocates.

But there are other valid methods. What should you do? Read about them and use the information to design a workout routine that suits your enthusiasm and time for weight training as well as your cycling objectives. Much more important than which approach you follow is that weight training is part of your program.

Strength and Aerobic Power

Most people used to think that cyclists were aerobic athletes, shot-putters were strength athletes, and never the twain should meet. But now the word is out that max VO_2, the lab test that measures maximal oxygen consumption and indicates cycling potential, is inseparable from leg strength. For proof, recall a day when your legs were tired from several consecutive hard rides and no matter how hard you tried, you couldn't elevate your heart rate. If you had taken a max-VO_2 test, the results would have been far below your potential.

Now suppose your legs felt fresh but lacked strength. You'd experience the same disheartening results. "If your legs are too weak to drive your heart and lungs to maximum levels, your max-VO_2 performance will be low," explains David Martin, exercise physiology researcher at the Olympic Training Center in Colorado Springs. "Strengthen the legs and you can improve your peak VO_2 and your cycling performance."

Peter Francis, Ph.D., renowned for his work in cycling biomechanics, agrees with this basic change in training philosophy. "The traditional approach to cycling was to ride a great deal," he says. "Now, we believe that cycling inefficiently only trains you to cycle inefficiently. We know that specific strength training is important."

Injury Prevention

The benefit of strength training is vital to racers and recreational riders who don't want the loss of fitness and health that injuries cause. Weight training strengthens the shoulder girdle and neck, helping you withstand overuse injuries and absorb crash impacts. A good leg program balances the strength of the opposing muscles—quadriceps and hamstrings—to help you avoid muscle pulls from hard efforts. Weight training is your injury insurance policy.

You need to lift wisely, however. Moderation is key to improvement and avoiding an injury in the weight room. Cyclists who don't overdo iron therapy don't lose their freshness, either. "The difference between fitness and fatigue is performance," says Martin. If your legs are dead from too much strength work, you won't benefit from time on the bike. Furthermore, he says, there's no need to fear loss of conditioning as you rest, since "fatigue is eliminated faster than fitness."

Remember, there's no cycling-related reason to build bulging biceps, and a 400-pound deadlift is useful only in hoisting your bike onto the roof rack. "Don't waste time doing more than necessary in the weight room," stresses Harvey Newton, a masters racer and a former U.S. Olympic weight-lifting coach. "Get in, do a cycling-specific strength workout, and then go on to something else."

The late Carl Leusenkamp, a national-team track coach, used to remind his riders, "Don't let weight training become an end in itself. Use weights to help you go faster on the bike."

Proper Planning

Early attempts at incorporating weight training into cycling programs often failed because they were badly planned. Know what you want from strength training before you begin. Each fall, formulate your goals for the coming year. "Look at the end of the riding season as the beginning of your year," advised Leusenkamp. "Evaluate and plan." A valuable tool is a training diary, which helps you assess your performance and stay motivated.

Athletes in all sports vary their training to avoid staleness and create periods of performance. "You need a long-range, year-round approach to training," explains Newton, "because a cyclist has only about 4 months to do serious strength training." He suggests starting in October with a transitional weight-training phase lasting about 4 weeks. By varying the exercises, by using light weights with a greater number of repetitions, and by working out 2 or 3 times per week, you'll accustom your muscles to lifting.

Ease gradually from riding to weight training because, as Dr. Francis warns, "The best predictor of injury is change."

Next comes a 4- to 6-week "hypertrophy," or preliminary strength-building, period. It features thrice-weekly workouts using three sets of each exercise done for 8 to 12 repetitions apiece. Both of these early phases are vital. "If you begin strength training without transitional and hypertrophy periods," warns Newton, "you'll get injured."

Only then are you ready for the meat of the program—4 to 6 weeks of basic strength development using five or more sets of each exercise with no more than eight reps apiece. Conclude with a month of power development by doing three or four sets of exercises specific to cycling (leg presses, stepups, lunges) using slightly higher reps (about 15) and greater speed of movement.

Afterward, don't let your hard-earned strength deteriorate during the riding season. Maintain it with pushups, pullups, and abdominal exercises at least twice a week. But don't forget that your priority is cycling. "When the season begins, it's not the time to set records in the weight room," says Newton.

Reconsidering Traditional Ways

When planning your training, don't repeat the mistakes of the past. For example, calf raises have traditionally been part of cycling weight programs. After all, when you ride behind someone with impressive calves, it looks as if they're vital to the pedal stroke. But "it's the quads that are actually flexing the foot," according to Dr. Francis. "The calf muscles act merely as a tight wire to transfer the quads' power to the foot and pedal." So, forgo the calf raises and focus on developing the quad power that really counts.

Circuit training has been similarly misinterpreted. It involves a series of light-weight/high-repetition exercises aimed at building muscle endurance and cardiovascular fitness. Recent research, however, indicates that its effect on aerobic fitness is minimal, especially for athletes who already are conditioned by endurance sports such as cycling. Because of this, Newton recommends using weights for their primary purpose—improving strength. "I recommend three to five sets of about 10 reps rather than high-rep training or circuits," he says.

There's no reason to spend hours in the weight room, even in midwinter. Six exercises packed into 30 minutes are all you need. Do an exercise for the quads such as leg presses or stepups, and leg curls for the hamstrings. Choose an upper-body pulling movement such as bentover rows, and a pushing exercise such as bench presses. Then add two "assistance" exercises such as abdominal crunches and back extensions. "Cyclists use lower-back muscles to keep from straightening up on powerful pedal strokes," explains Dr. Francis. "They also need strong abdominals to avoid back injuries."

One-Set Theory

Here's good news if you're a recreational cyclist simply looking for better muscle balance and tone along with some injury protection. Because you're not seeking maximum development from weight training, you can do just one set of each exercise and still get good results while saving time and energy.

That's the recent finding of researchers Ralph Carpinetti and Robert Otto, who say that in 33 of 35 studies, there was "no significant difference in strength increase between individuals performing single-set and those performing multiple-set exercise." Their conclusion: One set of four to six exercises, each with 8 to 12 reps, provides nearly the same benefit as doing 2 or more (up to as many as 15) sets of each exercise. If this method sounds good to you, use a weight that allows all reps in good form. When you can exceed 12 reps, increase the weight by about 3 percent.

Naturally, there are dissenters. Newton, for instance, points out that while single-set routines do work well in studies lasting 8 to 12 weeks, multiple sets are more effective over the longer duration of a typical winter program. There's also the warmup factor. Doing at least two sets lets you use a lighter weight the first time through before using the optimum weight.

Researcher Everett Harmon, Ph.D., advocates three sets total, contending that "muscles seem to need preparation to go all-out. Doing two preliminary sets of about 80 and 90 percent of the final weight works better."

The bottom line? If your energy, workout time, or interest in weight training is limited and your choice is between a minimal program or no program at all, go the one-set route. There will be noticeable improvement for the few minutes you spend each week. On the other hand, if you have the time and ambition, you should see even greater benefits from a multiple-set program.

Tips from a Top Coach

The Bulgarians have long been at the forefront of strength development. Their lifters have won Olympic and world titles disproportionate to their country's population, and their coaches have become leaders in applying the principles of strength development to other sports. Bulgarian national weight-lifting coach Angel Spassov offered some advice for cyclists during a U.S. lecture tour.

Be patient. Weight training is not a quick fix. Three weeks or even 3 months in the weight room won't elevate you from a century rider to Paris-Brest-Paris champion. "You need 6 to 8 years of training to be world class in any sport," according to Spassov. Your body will improve, but only on its own timetable. Forcing rapid improvement in cycling or weight training leads to injury, stalled progress, and staleness. "Always, when we break the laws of nature," he says, "we make mistakes."

Use technology. The same heart-rate monitor that's so valuable for training on the bike is also useful for winter weight workouts. When riding, you elevate your heart rate to near maximum during interval training and let it drop to about 120 beats per minute for recovery. Nearly the same principles apply to strength training. "In power sports," explains Spassov, "strength is best built in the 160 to 180 range. But let your heart rate drop much lower between sets."

Use weights to develop cycling-specific strength. Doing intervals up steep hills builds power. But so do leg presses—and they do it faster. "It's hard to use your sport to develop power to its fullest," says Spassov. "If you use an aerobic sport, it takes much longer. You need weights." For endurance cyclists, this supports the contention that upper-body strength can be developed better in the weight room than on the bike. Bench presses, rows, crunches, and back extensions are particularly effective at conditioning the muscles likely to fatigue during long rides.

Be aware of the link. Endurance doesn't exist separately from strength. For example, Spassov explains that a runner takes about 27,000 steps during a marathon and with each step pushes two times his body weight. That's about 1,600 tons over the 26 miles, so the need for strength is evident. In addition, Spassov maintains that while the marathon runner's heart rate returns to normal about 3 hours after the event and the blood profile is back at baseline in 3 days, the legs need about a month to recover. The more strength the legs possess, the faster the recovery.

Keep resistance low to maintain speed and technique. Work with 28 percent of your one-rep maximum to build endurance, Spassov recommends. For instance, if you can bench press 150 pounds one time, do multiple reps with 40 pounds to build endurance.

Step up to stepups. Squats have long been the cornerstone of strength programs, but they are no longer done in the Bulgarian system. "Squats put too much compression on the lower back," explains Spassov, "and there's no correlation between squat performance and sports performance." As a result, he substitutes a related exercise called stepups. This alternative is effective for the legs but easier on the back. Here's how to do it.

1. Face a bench. It should be high enough so that your thigh is parallel to the ground when you put a foot on it and stand on the toes of your rear foot.

2. Step up onto the bench. Don't push off with your rear leg; make sure the leg on the bench does all the work. Staying on the toes of your rear leg will ensure that it doesn't get involved.

3. Don't alternate legs after each rep. Instead, keep the same leg on the bench until you have done the planned number of reps, then switch legs.

4. Start the exercise using just your body weight as resistance. As you get stronger, hold a barbell or inner tube filled with sand over your shoulders. Don't use more weight than your maximum squat or leg-press weight divided by 2.2.

Mix weight training and cycling. In the early season, do easy warmups of 15 minutes on the bike or resistance trainer followed by several intervals of hard pedaling mixed with easy pedaling, Spassov recommends. Then get off the bike, change shoes, and do a short, intense program of leg development including stepups and leg presses. Get back on the bike and spin easily for 15 minutes to cool down. Mixing cycling and weight training in the same workout ensures that the strength you're building transfers to the specific movement of cycling. You'll keep your pedaling finesse as you get stronger.

21
Stationary Cycling

If you live north of the Sunbelt, you don't ride much in winter, do you? Perhaps you get out occasionally, but roads and trails covered by snow and ice aren't just tough to ride on, they can be dangerous. Then there's the windchill that's automatically caused by cycling, making even a calm day seem extra cold. To top it off, it gets dark early in winter. Even when conditions permit a ride, your daily schedule may not give you a chance before the 5:00 P.M. sunset. In this sense, Florida cyclists are not much better off than those who live in Minnesota.

But even in the most inhospitable places on the continent, cycling is always possible. Set up your bike on an indoor trainer, and nothing can stop you from retaining summer's fitness. Done right, three or four weekly sessions can actually increase your power and speed.

The enemy is boredom, but you can battle it with variety. Here are five indoor workouts that will help you pedal through the winter without brain drain. They're adapted from the book *Smart Cycling* by

Arnie Baker, M.D., a top masters competitor who is a member of *Bicycling* magazine's Fitness Advisory Board.

Note that the gearing recommendations in the following workouts are based on the common 39/53-tooth chainring combination found on road bikes, and a cassette (5-, 6-, 7-, 8-, and 9-speed will work) that includes cogs with 13, 15, 17, 19, and 21 teeth. If your gearing differs, use similar combinations and pay close attention to your perceived exertion to be sure you're not overdoing or underdoing it. If you don't have a cadence indicator on your cyclecomputer, count the revolutions of one foot for 15 seconds and multiply by four to determine rpm.

Variety

MINUTES	ACTIVITY
3	Spin easily in 39×21T; start at 70 rpm and increase by 10 rpm each minute
3	Increase gearing to 39×19T; start at 70 rpm; increase to 100 rpm for 15 seconds each minute
3	Shift to 53×17T and stand for 1 minute; then sit for 1 minute in 39×19T; then stand again in 53×17T
3	Shift to 53×19T; alternate between 100 rpm and 70 rpm every 30 seconds
8	In 39×19T, pedal with one leg for 1 minute; switch legs each minute
3	Spin easily in 39×19T
10	Pedal hard in 53×17T for 1 minute; then spin easily in 39×17T for 1 minute; repeat 5 times
8	Sprint in 53×15T for 15 seconds; then spin easily in 39×19T for 45 seconds; repeat 8 times
4	Cool down by spinning gently for just over a minute each in 39×17T, 19T, and 21T

Time Trial

MINUTES	ACTIVITY
12	Warm up with first 12 minutes of Activity in "Variety" workout
5	Shift to 53×19T and pedal steadily at 90–100 rpm
4	Spin easily in 39×19T
5	Shift to 53×17T and pedal hard at 90–100 rpm
5	Spin easily in 39×19T
10	Shift to 53×17T or 15T and pedal hard at 90–100 rpm
4	Cool down by spinning easily in 39×21T

Sprint

MINUTES	ACTIVITY
12	Warm up with first 12 minutes of Activity in "Variety" workout
10	Shift to 39×17T and spin at over 100 rpm for 10 seconds; then spin easily and slowly for 50 seconds; repeat 10 times
5	Spin slowly in 39×19T
10	Shift to 53×19T and sprint all-out for 10 seconds; then spin easily and slowly in 39×19T for 50 seconds; repeat 10 times
8	Cool down by spinning easily in 39×21T

Hillclimb

MINUTES	ACTIVITY
12	Warm up with first 12 minutes of Activity in "Variety" workout
2	Shift to 53×19T and pedal at 80 rpm
2	Recover in 39×19T
2	Shift to 53×17T and pedal at 80 rpm
2	Recover in 39×19T
2	Shift to 53×15T and pedal at 80 rpm
2	Recover in 39×19T
2	Shift to 53×13T and don't let your cadence drop below 70 rpm
6	Recover in 39×19T; you've earned it
20	Shift to 53×13T; pedal hard at 80 rpm for a minute; recover for a minute in 39×21T; repeat 10 times
3	Cool down by spinning easily in 39×21T

Recovery

MINUTES	ACTIVITY
12	Warm up with first 12 minutes of Activity in "Variety" workout
5	Spin easily in 39×17T after putting on your favorite CD
10	Spin in 39×15T as you hum along
5	Spin fast in 39×17T while listening to up-tempo tunes
10	Spin easily in 39×17T while playing slower stuff
3	Cool down in 39×21T as the album ends

Survival Tips

Use these five tips to make your journeys on the nowhere bike easier to endure.

1. Ventilate. Trapped in still air, you build an enormous amount of body heat on an indoor trainer. Crack a window and create an artificial headwind by placing a 24-inch box fan 3 feet in front of your face. You'll still drip, so wear a sweatband and wristbands. In case they overflow, have spares within reach. Wear a T-shirt to stop perspiration from flowing down your body. Put a towel over the bike, too, because sweat can damage the frame and components.

2. Hydrate. Drinking is important to keep your core temperature down and prevent cardiac drift—the elevated heart rate that occurs as blood thickens when plasma is lost through sweat. If you use a sports drink instead of water, you can also replace the energy you're burning. Drink at least one bottle (preferably chilled) during a 45-minute indoor session.

3. Keep it short. The drudgery outweighs the benefits of grinding away on the trainer in an attempt to build endurance. You can get a beneficial indoor workout in less than an hour. After that, you're into the realm of diminishing returns. Wait until you're back outside to do long rides.

4. Change your pace. Beat boredom by doing something different every minute or two. Stand up, change gears, increase cadence, alternate hand positions, pedal with one leg while resting the other foot on a stool—anything to add variety and take your mind off how slowly the hands on your clock are moving. This is why it helps to plan a specific workout instead of just climbing aboard to pedal.

5. Distract your mind. Some riders prefer Pearl Jam while others like watching bike-race videos. You can also find workout videos with programs to follow, and touring videos that put you in a pack of riders on scenic roads. Probably the ultimate solution is a Compu-Trainer. This sturdy stationary trainer has a control panel that connects to a TV through a modified Nintendo video-game system or to a personal computer. It displays heart rate, cadence, power output, calories burned, speed, and distance as you race various courses against an electronic opponent or your own previous performances. Resistance on your bike's rear wheel automatically changes for climbs and descents, making you shift gears just as you would on the real terrain. At more than $1,000, a CompuTrainer is expensive, but if you're confined to indoor cycling for long stretches and want to get

the most benefit possible, it may be the ticket. For information, check out the manufacturer's Web site at www.computrainer.com.

22
A Champion's Winter Program

You probably don't associate eastern Pennsylvania's Lehigh Valley with great training advances. Most cycling gurus have Italian names— Testa or Conconi—or they operate from Colorado Springs, plotting America's supersecret Olympic training programs. So how do you explain Marty Nothstein?

Nothstein, who grew up in the shadow of the Lehigh Valley Velodrome in tiny Trexlertown, won two 1994 world track championships following a winter hampered by atrocious weather. A key to this success was his coach, Gilbert "Gibby" Hatton, who developed a supercharged indoor winter training program that helped Nothstein develop speed, power, endurance, and the ability to recover quickly. This unique program combines weight training, indoor cycling, and swimming in what first appears as being too much for recreational cyclists, who must match merely mortal talent with careers (or school) and families.

But before the 1995 season, a group of masters racers participated in Hatton's program and showed that it can be combined with a busy off-bike life and still produce stellar results. This chapter will explain how you, too, can benefit. Hatton includes several training techniques discussed elsewhere in this book, combining them into a winter program that will help make each new season your best yet

One guy who can vouch for it is Dave Madden, an advertising executive in his mid-thirties. Even though he is also a dedicated runner and chained to a work schedule that involves travel nearly every week, Madden jumped from category 4 bike racing to category 2 in one season. In 1995, he placed in every masters 30-to-34 event he entered. Worried about endurance after a winter of Hatton's prescription of short, intense indoor rides, Madden began the next season with the

92-mile Rose Bowl Road Race. He made the first three breaks, which failed to stay away, and still had enough strength to solo away from the chase group in the last 5 miles.

Another believer is Tom Kellogg of Spectrum Cycles. With a thriving frame-building business and family, Kellogg's biggest enemy is time. "The group workouts made me fit," he says. "I was able to train consistently all winter, and the camaraderie of the group was a great bonus." Kellogg, in his upper forties, competes regularly in short, fast criterium races.

Here are the components of this powerful plan that has helped Nothstein win world championships and also boosted the performances of regular guys such as Madden and Kellogg.

Weights

Although traditional cycling coaches derided weight training for decades, we now know that it will make you a faster, more efficient cyclist.

Consider a study from the University of Illinois at Chicago. Eight experienced runners lifted three times per week for 10 weeks. They did three to five sets of squats, leg extensions, hamstring curls, and calf raises using a weight heavy enough to allow only about five reps per set. Not only did their leg strength increase 30 percent without any increase in muscle bulk but also their time to exhaustion on a cycling ergometer (at a hard 88 percent of maximum heart rate) increased 20 percent. Researchers theorize that weight training increases the strength of individual muscle cells, so the body requires fewer fibers—and less oxygen—at a given speed.

It's no surprise that strength training is central to Hatton's program. In fact, Madden calls it "the most important component."

Nothstein's personal strength coach is John Graham of the Allentown Sports Medicine and Human Performance Center. Graham, who learned weight-training basics as a football player at the University of Pittsburgh, credits his refinements to Ed Burke, Ph.D., cycling physiologist and director of the exercise-science program at the University of Colorado at Colorado Springs; and Harvey Newton, a masters racer and a former U.S. Olympic weight-lifting coach. The weight program has six phases that concentrate on the winter season and then extend the benefits to the whole training year. It's a fully periodized approach that doesn't bore cyclists or bog their progress at long plateaus.

Phase 1: Adjust to Strength Work

Exercises: 10 or more

Sets: 1 to 3

Reps: 12 to 20

Intensity: Minimal

Days per week: 2 or 3

This transition from the cycling season to more emphasis on weights usually occurs in October. The idea is to balance development between your upper and lower body. "We had sprinters who could squat 400 pounds," Graham says, "but they couldn't press 150." He also tests riders for muscle-group imbalances. For instance, cyclists typically have stronger quads than hamstrings, so Graham prescribes one-leg curls to address the discrepancy.

It's important to use weights that are light enough to permit as many as 20 reps per set. Don't worry about how much weight others are using. This is a good time to try varied exercises. For instance, if you always do leg presses on a machine, learn to do squats with free weights. Do a variety of upper- and lower-body exercises, including back extensions, leg presses, leg curls, calf raises, bench presses, seated rows, and abdominal work.

Phase 2: Build Muscle Tissue

Exercises: 9 or 10

Sets: 3

Reps: 8 to 12

Intensity: Moderate

Days per week: 3

From the first of November to mid-December is the developmental stage. Cut the number of exercises and prepare your muscles for the more intense work to come. Concentrate on specific muscle groups such as quads, glutes, calves, biceps, triceps, abdominals, back, and shoulders. Exercises include pullovers, dumbbell shoulder presses, dumbbell shrugs, squats or leg presses, biceps curls, and pullups. Use 60 to 70 percent of the maximum weight you can lift for one repetition.

Phase 3: Gain Strength

Exercises: 3 to 5

Sets: 4 to 6

Reps: 6 to 10

Intensity: Heavy

Days per week: 3

From mid-December to the end of January, concentrate on basic strength. "We use fewer reps but more explosion," says Graham. "Lower the weight slowly but go fast in the lifting phase." A typical workout includes incline presses, one-arm rows, bench presses, low pulley rows, dumbbell curls, and abdominal work. Alternate this workout with ones that include squats, upright rows, deadlifts, leg curls, calf raises, and back extensions. During this phase, use weights that are 80 to 90 percent of the maximum you can lift for one repetition.

Phase 4: Develop Explosive Power

Exercises: 3 or 4

Sets: 5

Reps: 4 to 10

Intensity: Moderate

Days per week: 2 or 3

During February, concentrate on cycling muscles by doing such exercises as partial squats, lunges, leg presses, leg curls, or rowing. Use weights that are 60 to 75 percent of your one-rep maximum.

Phase 5: Work on Muscular Endurance

Exercises: 6

Sets: 1 or 2

Reps: 12 to 15

Intensity: Low

Days per week: 2

This phase for March is only for riders who are kept off their bikes by bad early-season weather. If you're able to get outside for aerobic riding,

do that instead. Otherwise, Graham prescribes these exercises for the cycling muscle groups: leg presses, calf raises, bench presses, rowing,
pushups, and abdominal exercises. Reps should be done using light
weights (40 to 60 percent of your one-rep maximum) for 30 seconds,
with 30 seconds of rest between exercises.

Phase 6: Maintain Strength

Exercises: 4

Sets: 1 or 2

Reps: 10 to 12

Intensity: Moderate

Days per week: 1 or 2

Now you must maintain your upper-body strength during the season.
Focus on muscle groups not directly active during riding, including
your abdominals, lower back, arms, and shoulders. You can do this with
crunches, back extensions, pushups, and pullups if you're traveling and
don't have access to weight equipment. Otherwise, use 70 to 80 percent
of your one-rep maximum for exercises such as presses, bench presses,
shrugs, and bent rows.

Wheels

When Hatton's riders hammer the indoor road, they mount their bikes
on high-tech indoor trainers. Using your own bike instead of an ergometer (stationary bike) lets you maintain correct position while you
pedal through the winter. Advanced trainers such as the CompuTrainer
or any other model that provides wattage readings and other performance feedback help you track your efforts and avoid boredom.

Maintaining intensity is the key to these workouts. "I'd never trained
at such high intensity levels in winter before I got on Gibby's program,"
says Madden. "The indoor trainer sessions were almost like a hard
group ride."

The traditional off-season advice is to build endurance, then concentrate on speed later in the spring. But Hatton contends that short, intense winter workouts fit into most riders' schedules better than long
grinds. More important, he says, strength and power are hard to build,
while endurance is relatively easy. By beginning to develop speed in
winter, you have more time to concentrate on it.

This part of the program uses three cycles, each 6 weeks long, aimed at developing a specific energy system. Begin in October and continue into February.

Cycle 1: Power

Focus: High-resistance, fast-cadence workouts with intervals from 30 seconds to 3 minutes

Sample workout: Warm up for 15 minutes in progressively larger gears until your heart rate is about 80 percent of maximum. Then begin a ladder with 30-second steps. Start with 30 seconds of hard effort followed by 1 minute of easy spinning. The next hard effort is 60 seconds (a "step up the ladder," or increase of 30 seconds), followed by another minute of easy spinning. Continue this pattern until the hard effort is 3 minutes, then follow the ladder back down to 30 seconds. Always allow 1 minute between steps for recovery. During the hard efforts, keep your cadence at 90 rpm or more and your heart rate at 80 to 90 percent of max.

Cycle 2: Endurance

Focus: Low-resistance, moderate-cadence workouts with heart rates as low as 75 percent of max and intervals as long as 12 minutes

Sample workout: You don't need to emphasize endurance in winter, but you don't want to ignore it, either. Warm up as in Cycle 1. Then do three sets of 10-minute efforts at 75 percent of max heart rate and a cadence of 85 to 95 rpm. Spin easily for 3 minutes between sets.

Cycle 3: Speed

Focus: High-intensity sprints shorter than 45 seconds

Sample workout: Warm up as in Cycle 1. Do 10 all-out sprints of 20 seconds each, using the biggest gear and fastest cadence you can. Spin a low gear for 5 minutes between sprints to achieve full recovery. Finish by spinning easily for 15 minutes to cool down.

Water

For most of us, this is probably the toughest component of Hatton's program to commit to. Mixing three weekly swimming sessions into your winter training can be logistically difficult unless you join an athletic club that has a weight room, pool, and stationary trainers. If there isn't a complete facility in your area, perhaps you can combine clubs or do some of the training at home.

If you can't find a pool, it's okay to skip these water workouts. Some of Hatton's masters riders just did the weights and stationary cycling. The program can work with only two components, but Hatton says that maximum improvement depends on swimming.

Madden, who joined in the pool sessions, agrees. "It produces an aerobic workout without beating up the legs; and it's different from riding, so it's a mental break."

Riders typically swim an hour, doing warmup laps followed by intervals. Sometimes they use a kickboard. These workouts are combined with stationary-cycling sessions. Here's a sample workout.

1. Warm up by swimming easily for 10 minutes.

2. Do 10 sets of two laps at a brisk crawl, followed by 10 sets of one lap with a kickboard.

3. Cool down in the pool, then move to the bike and do the "Cycle 2: Endurance" workout.

Putting It All Together

Hatton's final advice is that you shouldn't do this program by yourself. It's possible, but it probably won't be as effective.

"It's easier to train hard when someone's barking at you," Madden found.

"The most important part was having a group to train with," adds Kellogg. "If all the guys were meeting at 5:30, I'd be there. Otherwise, I might just keep working at the shop."

A strong group provides inspiration in other ways, too. "Gibby had us doing 20-second sprints, and we were dying," said one participant. "But over on the next trainer, Nothstein was doing 160 rpm at 1,200 watts, and nothing was moving except his legs. It was inspiring."

This program is tough. Mold it to your personal situation and equipment, then do as well as you can. Next spring, you'll be a stronger and faster cyclist for it. If you're afraid of burnout or are a recreational rider not willing to commit so much time and effort, scale back the volume and intensity of the workouts.

When you combine all three elements, here's what a typical midwinter training week looks like. The cross-training can consist of light recreational exercise such as running, hiking, cross-country skiing, snowshoeing, basketball—something that's fun and gets your body moving.

Sunday: Weights and low-intensity cross-training

Monday: Easy pedaling or cross-training for recovery

Tuesday: Easy warmup on the trainer, then weights

Wednesday: Swim for an hour, followed by interval program on the trainer

Thursday: Repeat Wednesday

Friday: Repeat Monday

Saturday: Repeat Wednesday

Road Riding Position

1. **Arms:** Beware road rider's rigor mortis. Keep your elbows bent and relaxed to absorb shock and prevent veering when you hit a bump. Keep your arms in line with your body, not splayed to the side, to make a more compact, aerodynamic package.

2. **Upper body/shoulders:** The operative words: Be still. Imagine the calories burned by rocking from side to side with every pedal stroke on a 25-mile ride. Use that energy for pedaling. Also, beware of creeping forward on the saddle and hunching your back when tired. Periodically shift to a higher gear and stand to pedal to prevent stiffness in your hips and back.

3. **Head and neck:** Avoid putting your head down, especially when you're tired. Periodically tilt your head from side to side to stretch and relax neck muscles.

4. **Hands:** Change hand position frequently to prevent finger numbness and upper-body stiffness. A white-knuckle hold on the handlebar is

unnecessary and will produce energy-sapping muscle tension throughout your arms and shoulders. Grasp the drops for descents or high-speed riding, and the brake lever hoods for relaxed cruising. On long climbs, hold the top of the bar to sit upright and open your chest for easier breathing. When standing, grasp the hoods lightly and gently rock the bike from side to side in synch with your pedal strokes. Always keep your thumbs and a finger of each hand closed around the hoods or bar to prevent losing hold on an unexpected bump.

5. **Handlebar:** Bar width should equal shoulder width. Err on the side of a wider one to open your chest for breathing. Some models are available with a large drop (vertical distance) to help big hands fit into the hooks. Position the flat, bottom portion of the bar horizontally or pointed slightly down toward the rear brake.

6. **Brake levers:** Levers can be moved around the curve of the bar to give you the best compromise between holding the hoods and braking when your hands are in the bar hooks. Most riders do best if the lever tips touch a straightedge extended forward from under the flat, bottom portion of the bar.

7. **Stem height:** With the stem high enough (normally about an inch below the top of the saddle), you'll be more inclined to use the drops. Putting it lower can improve aerodynamics but may be uncomfortable. Never position the stem above its maximum-extension line (usually etched in the side of the stem), or your weight on the bar could cause it to break.

8. **Top-tube and stem length:** These combined dimensions, which determine your reach, vary according to your flexibility and anatomy. There is no ultimate prescription, but there is a good starting point: When you're comfortably seated with your elbows slightly bent and your hands on the brake hoods, the front hub should be obscured by the handlebar. This is a relatively upright position, and with time you may benefit from a longer stem extension to improve aerodynamics and flatten your back.

9. **Back:** A flat back is the defining mark of a pro rider. The correct stem and top-tube combination is crucial for this, but so is hip flexibility. Concentrate on rotating the top of your hips forward. Think of trying to touch the top tube with your stomach. This image will help stop you from rounding your back.

10. **Saddle height:** There are various formulas for this, but you needn't be a mathematician to know what the correct height looks like. Your knees should be slightly bent at the bottom of the pedal stroke, and your hips shouldn't rock on the saddle (when viewed from behind). Try this quick method, which is used at the Olympic Training Center in Colorado Springs: Set the height so there is 5 mm of clearance between your heel and the pedal at the bottom of the stroke. Add a few mm if your shoes have very thin soles at the heels compared to at the forefeet. Raise the saddle 2 or 3 mm if you have long feet in proportion to your height. For those who have knee pain caused by chondromalacia, a softening or wearing away and cracking of the cartilage under the kneecap that results in pain and inflammation, a saddle on the higher side of the acceptable range can be therapeutic. Gradually raise it until hip rocking begins, then lower it slightly. Make saddle height changes 2 mm at a time to avoid leg strain.

11. **Saddle tilt:** The saddle should be level, which you can check by laying a straightedge along its length. A slight downward tilt may be more comfortable if you're using an extreme forward position with an aero bar and elbow rests, but too much causes you to slide forward and place excessive weight on your arms.

12. **Fore/aft saddle position:** The trend is to move the saddle back to produce more power for climbing. To start with, sit comfortably in the center of the saddle with the crankarms horizontal. Drop a plumb line from the front of your forward kneecap. It should touch the end of the crankarm. This is the neutral position, and you should be able to achieve it by loosening the seatpost clamp and sliding the saddle fore or aft. Climbers, time trialists, and some road racers prefer the line to fall a couple of centimeters behind the end of the crankarm to increase leverage in big gears. Conversely, track and criterium racers like a more forward position to improve leg speed. Remember, if your reach to the handlebar is wrong, use stem length, not fore/aft saddle position, to correct it.

13. **Frame:** Measure your inseam from crotch to floor with your bare feet 6 inches apart, then multiply by 0.65. This equals your road-

frame size, measured along the seat tube from the center of the crankset axle to the center of the top tube. As a double check, this should produce 4 to 5 inches of exposed seatpost when your saddle height is correct. (The post's maximum-extension line shouldn't show, of course.)

14. **Butt:** By sliding rearward or forward on the saddle, you can emphasize different muscle groups. This can be useful on a long climb. Moving forward emphasizes the quadriceps muscle, on the fronts of your thighs, while moving back accentuates the opposite side, your hamstrings and glutes.

15. **Feet:** Notice your footprints as you walk from a swimming pool. Some of us are pigeon-toed and others are duck-footed. To prevent knee injury, strive for a cleat position that accommodates your natural foot angle. Make cleat adjustments on rides until you feel right, or pay a shop to do it using a fitting device. Better still, use a clipless pedal system that allows your feet to pivot freely ("float"), thus making precise adjustment unnecessary. Position cleats fore/aft so the widest part of each foot is directly above or slightly in front of the pedal axle.

16. **Crankarm length:** The trend is toward longer levers. These add power but may inhibit pedaling speed. In general, if your inseam is less than 29 inches, use 165-mm crankarms; if it's from 29 to 32 inches, 170 mm; from 32 to 34 inches, 172.5; and more than 34 inches, 175 mm. Crankarm length is measured from the center of the fixing bolt to the center of the pedal mounting hole. It's usually stamped on the back of the arm.

Mountain Biking Position

1. **Frame:** Spontaneous (sometimes unwanted) dismounts are a part of riding off-road. Consequently, you need lots of clearance between you and the top tube. The ideal mountain bike size is about 4 inches smaller than your road bike size. This isn't as critical if you'll be riding only on pavement or smooth dirt roads, but there's no advantage to having a frame any larger than the smallest size that provides enough saddle height and reach to the handlebar. Smaller frames are lighter, stiffer, and more maneuverable. Because manufacturers specify frame size in different ways, use the stand-over test. When straddling the bike while wearing your riding shoes, there should be a minimum of 4 inches between your crotch and the top tube.

2. **Saddle height:** Seatpost lengths of 350 mm are common, so a lot of post can be out of the frame before the maximum-extension line (etched on the post) shows. For efficient pedaling, your knee should

remain slightly bent at the bottom of the pedal stroke (the same as with a road bike). However, you may wish to lower the saddle slightly for rough terrain, enabling you to rise up so the bike can float beneath you without pounding your crotch. On steep descents, some riders drop the saddle even farther to keep their weight low and rearward, but others just slide their butts off the back.

3. **Saddle tilt:** Most off-road riders prefer a level saddle, but some (including many women) find a slight nose-down tilt avoids pressure and irritation. Others go slightly nose-up, which helps them sit back and lessens strain on their arms.

4. **Fore/aft saddle position:** This variable is not for adjusting your reach to the handlebar—that's why stems come with different extensions. Use the same procedure described for roadies on page 107.

5. **Stem:** Mountain bike stems come in a huge variety of extensions (from 60 to 150 mm) and rises (from -5 to +25 degrees). For good control, the stem should place the bar an inch or two below the top of the saddle. This helps put weight on the front wheel so it's easier to steer on climbs and the wheel is less likely to leave the ground. Never exceed the stem's maximum-height line, or it could break and cause a nasty crash. The extension should allow comfortably bent arms and a straight back. A longer and lower reach works for fast

Hints for Hybrids

Hybrids (also known as cross bikes) generally have 700C wheels like road bikes but flat handlebars like mountain bikes. They are close to road bikes for most dimensions. However, you may wish to select a frame size at the small end of your acceptable range if you'll be riding it off-road, for greater crotch clearance. Some hybrids also have higher bottom brackets than road bikes, which means their stand-over heights are less for identical-size road frames. Strive for at least 2 inches of clearance between your crotch and the top tube.

Many hybrids also come with short, high-rise stems, supplying an upright position for casual riding. In time, you may wish to purchase a longer stem with less rise to get closer to the ideal, 45-degree back angle described in the advice for fitting a mountain bike.

cruising, but a higher, closer hand position affords more control on difficult trails.

6. **Handlebar width:** An end-to-end measurement of 21 to 24 inches is common. If the bar seems too wide, it can be trimmed with a hacksaw or pipe cutter. First, though, move your controls and grips inward and take a ride to make sure you'll like the new width. And remember to leave a bit extra at each end if you use bar-ends. In general, the narrower the handlebar, the quicker the steering. Wider bars provide more control at slow speed.

7. **Handlebar sweep:** Flat bars can be straight or have up to 11 degrees of rearward bend per side. The choice is strictly one of arm and wrist comfort. Be aware that changing the sweep also changes your reach to the grips and could require a different stem length. Also available are bars with an upward bend or rise. These can allow a lower stem position.

8. **Bar-ends:** These are great for getting climbing leverage and achieving a longer, lower position on flat fire roads or pavement. Angle them slightly upward. Models that curve inward help protect your hands and are less likely to snag brush on tight singletrack. If you're thinking of installing bar-ends, make sure your handlebar can accept them. Some ultralight bars can't.

9. **Crankarm length:** Manufacturers usually vary this with frame size. For greater leverage on steep climbs, a mountain bike typically comes with crankarms 5 mm longer than would a road bike for the same size rider.

10. **Arms:** Slightly bent arms act as shock absorbers. If you can only reach the bar with straight elbows, get a shorter stem or condition yourself to lean forward more by rotating your hips.

11. **Back:** When your top-tube/stem-length combo is correct, you should have a forward lean of about 45 degrees during normal riding. This is an efficient angle because the strong gluteus muscles of your buttocks don't contribute much to pedaling when you're sitting more upright. Plus, a forward lean shifts some weight to your arms, so your butt doesn't get as sore.

12. Upper body: Don't hunch your shoulders and you'll avoid muscle soreness and fatigue. Tilt your head every few minutes to stave off tight neck muscles.

13. Hands and wrists: Grasp the bar just firmly enough to maintain control. Set the brake levers close to the grips and angle them so you can extend a finger or two around each and still hold the bar comfortably. Your wrists should be straight when you're standing over the saddle and braking, as on a downhill. Always ride with your thumbs under the bar so your hands can't slip off.

Glossary

A

Aerobic: Exercise at an intensity that allows the body's need for oxygen to be continually met. This intensity can be sustained for long periods.

Anaerobic: Exercise above the intensity at which the body's need for oxygen can be met. This intensity can be sustained only briefly.

Anaerobic threshold (AT): *See* Lactate threshold.

B

Bonk: To run out of energy, usually because the rider has failed to eat or drink enough.

BPM: Abbreviation for "beats per minute" in reference to heart rate.

C

Cadence: The number of times during 1 minute that a pedal stroke is completed. Also called pedal rpm.

Carbohydrate: In the diet, it is broken down to glucose, the body's principal energy source, through digestion and metabolism. Carb can be simple (sugars) or complex (bread, pasta, grains, fruits, vegetables); the latter type contains additional nutrients. One gram of carbohydrate supplies four calories.

Century: A ride of 100 miles or 100 kilometers (called a metric century).

Chondromalacia: A softening or wearing away and cracking of the cartilage under the kneecap, resulting in pain and inflammation.

Circuit training: A weight-training technique in which you move rapidly from exercise to exercise with no rest.

Criterium: A short-course road race featuring numerous laps with tight turns. It puts a premium on cornering and sprinting ability.

Cross-training: Combining sports for mental refreshment and physical conditioning, especially during cycling's off-season.

D

Downshift: To shift to a lower gear, that is, to a larger cog or smaller chainring.

Draft: The slipstream created by a moving rider. Another rider close behind can keep the same pace using about 20 percent less energy.

E

Ergometer: A stationary device typically found in human-performance labs. It is pedaled like a bicycle and may measure power output in watts. Resistance comes from friction against a large flywheel.

F

Fat: In the diet, it is the most concentrated source of food energy, supplying nine calories per gram. Stored fat provides about half the energy required for low-intensity exercise.

Fixed gear: A single-speed drivetrain that does not allow coasting. When the bike rolls, the crankset turns. It is used on track bikes and sometimes for early-season road training.

G

Glutes: The gluteal muscles of the buttocks. They are key to pedaling power.

Glycogen: A fuel derived as glucose (sugar) from carbohydrate and stored in the muscles and liver. It's the primary energy source for high-intensity cycling. Reserves are normally depleted after about 2½ hours of riding.

Glycogen window: The period within an hour after exercise, when depleted muscles are most receptive to restoring their glycogen content. During this time, eating foods or drinking fluids rich in carbohydrate enhances energy stores and recovery.

Granny gear: The lowest gear ratio, combining the small chainring with the largest cassette cog. It's mainly used for very steep climbs.

H

Hamstrings: The muscles on the back of the thighs, which are not well-developed by cycling.

I

Interval training: A type of workout in which periods of intense effort are alternated with periods of easy effort for recovery.

L

Lactate: *See* Lactic acid.

Lactate threshold (LT): The exertion level at which the body can no longer produce energy aerobically, resulting in the buildup of lactic acid. This is marked by muscle fatigue, pain, and shallow, rapid breathing. The heart rate at which this occurs is termed LTHR. Also called anaerobic threshold (AT).

Lactic acid: A substance formed during anaerobic metabolism when there is incomplete breakdown of glucose. It rapidly produces muscle fatigue and pain. Also called lactate.

M

Max VO₂: The maximum amount of oxygen that can be consumed during all-out exertion. This is a key indicator of a person's potential in cycling and other aerobic sports. It's largely genetically determined but can be improved somewhat by training.

O

Overtraining: Long-lasting physical and mental fatigue resulting from the stress of too much work without enough rest.

P

Pedal rpm: *See* Cadence.

Periodization: The process of dividing training into specific phases by weeks or months.

Power: The combination of speed and strength.

Protein: In the diet, it is required for tissue growth and repair. Composed of structural units called amino acids, protein is not a significant energy source unless enough calories and carbohydrate are consumed. One gram of protein equals four calories.

Pushing: Pedaling with a relatively slow cadence, using larger gears.

Q

Quadriceps: The muscle group on the fronts of the thighs, which are well-developed by cycling.

R

Repetition: Also called rep. In weight or interval training, each individual exertion. For example, if you press a barbell five times or do a series of five sprints, you are doing five reps.

Resistance trainer: A stationary training device into which the bike is clamped. Pedaling resistance increases with pedaling speed to simulate actual riding. Also known as an indoor, wind, or mag trainer. The last two names are derived from the fan or magnet that creates resistance on the rear wheel.

Rollers: A stationary training device consisting of three or four long cylinders connected by belts. Both bike wheels roll on these cylinders so that balancing is much like actual riding.

S

Set: In weight or interval training, one group of repetitions. For example, if you do eight reps three times you are doing three sets.

Speed: The ability to accelerate quickly and maintain a very fast cadence for brief periods.

Speedwork: A general term for intervals and other high-velocity training, such as sprints and time trials.

Spinning: Pedaling with a relatively fast cadence using low to moderate gears.

U

Upshift: To shift to a higher gear, that is, to a smaller cog or larger chainring.

Index

Underscored page references indicate boxed text.
Boldface references indicate photographs.